ANDERSON JANE
CW00694316

# Dream... Do it!

NORTH EAST LINCOLNSHIRE
LIBRARIES
WITHDRAWN
FROM STOCK
AUTHORISED:

# *Dream it* Do it!

***How dreams can change your life for the better – and forever***

JANE ANDERSON BSc HONS

Angus&Robertson
An imprint of HarperCollins*Publishers*

**Angus&Robertson**
An imprint of HarperCollinsPublishers

First published in Australia in 1995



**HarperCollins*Publishers***
25 Ryde Road, Pymble, Sydney, NSW 2073, Australia
31 View Road, Glenfield, Auckland 10, New Zealand
77-85 Fulham Palace Road, London W6 8JB, United Kingdom
Hazelton Lane, 55 Avenue Road, Suite 2900, Toronto, Ontario M5R 3L2
and 1995 Markham Road, Scarborough, Ontario M1B 5M8, Canada
10 East 53rd Street, New York NY 10032, USA

National Library of Australia Cataloguing-in-Publication data:

Anderson, Jane, 1954-.
Dream it; do it!

ISBN 0207 18875 0

1 Dreams - Case studies.
2. Life change events — Miscellanea. I. Title.

154.634

Cover illustration by J. F. Podevin/The Image Bank
Printed in Australia by Griffin Paperbacks

9 8 7 6 5 4 3 2 1 95 96 97 98 99

# CONTENTS

## On Precognition 111

## On Realising Potential 142

# ACKNOWLEDGEMENTS

My most humble thanks are extended to all the dreamers whose life-changing stories have been woven between the pages of this book. You have entrusted me with confidential material, much of which had not yet been expressed to many of your close relations, spouses or friends. It seems strange to think that we might pass each other on the street as strangers, since I have met few of you in person. For your trust, for placing your confidence in me to do justice to your experiences, and for the sheer time, labour, thought and emotional energy which you all devoted towards the creation of this book, I thank you.

Thank you also to all the radio stations and newspapers, too numerous to mention here by name, for your interest and enthusiastic support in publicising my work. Without your help I would not have come to know many of these dreamers, and their personal stories would remain untold.

Special thanks are extended to ABC radio presenter Paul Lineham (QLD's 612:4QR) and ABC metropolitan radio throughout NSW for their entertaining encouragement and intelligent support during my weekly Dream Talkback segments. They have played an important part in linking me with some of the people who contributed towards this book, as have many of the behind-the-scenes producers.

Thank you to all the dreamers who have added their perspectives, insights and experiences or who have challenged my understanding over the years, through classes, discussions, workshops, radio programs and The Dream Research Bank.

But most of all, of course, I gratefully acknowledge the love and support of my husband, Glenn, and children, Rowan and Euan, for doing all the wonderful things they do and for knowing how to live with a writer on a deadline!

# Dedication

*To Glenn, Rowan and Euan for being living proof that dreams can and do change your life.*

# Preface

## River of Dreams

I came upon a river, perhaps no more than three or four metres wide, tumbling, lively, dispersing spangles of sunlight as it washed its way through mountainous soil. Up here, amongst the peaks, it was spring.

Stepping into the river I slipped beneath the surface, feeling its fresh yet warming waters flow across my skin. It seemed no miracle that I could easily breathe down here, surrounded by crystal water. I swam, froggy style, easily and with overwhelming tranquillity, following the river bed, observing every rock, colour, animal and plant along the way. The river was not deep and occasionally my knees touched the sand, reminding me to refine my swimming style.

And so I journeyed, neither needing to come up for air nor wishing to. (I, whose heartbeat races at the thought of being submerged in my waking life!) In time I came to the place where the river spurted into a waterfall, where its inner silence was transformed into a noisy, splendiferous sight, every drop that once slid within the body of the river now turned inside out, flung into the air, on the outside, for all to witness. Thousands would gaze upon the waterfall, perceiving the view from many angles and from great distances. Here, where the river splayed itself into the world, I need follow no longer.

Turning, I swam back and on past the point of entry, peacefully flowing, now heading upstream to find the source of the river, its origins. Satisfied, I turned again, finally to emerge at my own starting point.

I repeated this process through twenty-five different rivers, then lay content in the sunlight to absorb.

Within each dream lies life-changing potential which, if acted upon, can bestow anything from minor life improvements to total personal transformation. This was the premise of my first book, *Sleep On It and Change Your Life,* which was based on an in-depth survey of 160 dreamers over a period of a year. Shortly after its publication, I felt the need to reach out and find people whose life-changing dream stories could be told in greater personal detail, and also to open myself to further research into what makes any particular dream truly transformative.

When I dreamed the 'River of Dreams' I had already prepared much of the work for this book and was at the stage of deciding how to present it. I knew that I wanted to tell many of the dreamer's stories in greater detail, but I was also aware of my publisher's word-length requirements.

I awoke straight after this dream knowing exactly what it meant. There was no need for interpretation. Each river was one dreamer's story. Water often symbolises the emotions or the subconscious, and the river itself can be seen as the 'flow of life'. I knew I should present twenty-five life-changing stories in detail and then dip my hand into the ocean, into which all rivers run, to retrieve insights from the rest.

The dream suggested that I should enter each dreamer's life around the middle of the river, which I perceived as being the moment of the life-changing dream itself. Each story in this book therefore opens with the life-changing dream in question.

After immersion in the dream, re-living the dream experience as each dreamer had, mine was then the task to follow their lives both to the point where each changed life burst forth into the world (the waterfall) and to the place of origin, the source of each dreamer's tale. While I should observe and experience the full length of each story, my dream advised me not to go too deep: my occasional grazing of my knee on the river bed reminded me, symbolically, to tighten and refine my writing style, to view the overall span of the tale rather than its depth.

My dream reference to not coming up for air was a reassuring one for me, since my deadline was not far away. The tranquillity of each swim gave me the faith that I could write the book smoothly, with great concentration, in a limited amount of time, and that I would not feel the need to come up for air. Through holding this picture in my mind I was able to peacefully apply myself in concentrated periods that, years ago, would have caused me tremendous stress. Ah, the value of a dream!

Halfway through writing the book, I felt the need to add a detailed life-changing dream of my own, but anonymously, because it involves other people whose identity should remain hidden in respect for their private lives. You will discover, therefore, that I have swum twenty-five rivers — plus one, and taken nineteen invigorating dips into the great collective ocean of life to bring you this book.

On reviewing my own dream, 'River of Dreams', I laughed to see that even the significance of my 'froggy' swimming style was symbolically important. Frogs, in dreams, often symbolise transformation, since tadpoles metamorphose into frogs, and, far more importantly, ugly frogs transform into handsome princes! This book is the story of the transformation of forty-five people's lives through their dreams, but, unlike the fairytale of the princess and the frog-prince, these stories are true.

# Have You Ever Had a Dream Which Changed Your Life?

Well, have you?

Every dream is potentially life-changing, and at a rate of about five dreams a night (yes: we all dream and you can learn how to recall them all!) for 365 nights a year, more than 1,800 opportunities to improve your lot have flicked behind your closed eyelids for every year of your life. The only difference between the dreamers in this book and those who answered 'no' to the opening question, is … what? That's what I wanted to know, and that's where this story begins.

First I had to find people who had taken life-changing action because of a dream. Through 'The Dream Research Bank' I had access to a number of people who had life-changing dream stories to tell. The Dream Research Bank is an ever increasing network of people throughout Australia who keep in contact with my dream research through a quarterly publication, 'DreamNet'. This provides details of various research projects which members can take part in and areas of dream experience I am interested in collecting, alongside informative items on dreaming.

I was keen to attract a broad range of life-changing dream stories, so I increased the invitation through a publicity drive in early January 1995, calling for people who had had 'a dream which has changed your life somehow, for better or for worse', through a large number of radio and newspaper interviews across Australia. The response was immediate and very encouraging, and it was not long before I had identified all the contributors and despatched the initial questionnaire to each one.

The questionnaire (see page 14) was comprised of twelve simple questions which the dreamers were invited to answer in whatever detail they felt appropriate. My approach was to pose questions which interested me, but not to request tight, statistically accessible replies. I wanted each person to feel free to tell their own story within the loose guidelines of my questions, while also giving me points of reference to make comparisons and draw conclusions about the material as a whole. In retrospect, I feel this was a worthwhile method which enhanced the individuality of each story as well as allowing each dreamer's personality to add his or her own hue.

I decided not to give a precise definition of what I meant by a 'life-changing dream'. I left it open to people to decide for themselves what they considered to be 'life changing': if you've changed your life because of a dream, you know it — you don't need someone to define it for you. As Beth, one of the contributors to the book, said, 'Giving up smoking was a really big thing for me, so I am sure it's classified as life changing', while for others, such as Nellie, Sarras and Dee, 'life changing' is a rather mild way of saying 'life saving'. Nellie's dream returned her from the point of death, Sarras's dream experience renewed her will to live after aborting a suicide plan, and Dee had actually died, had her dream experience, and then been resuscitated to live a changed life.

I realised that asking people for unstructured written replies could be too time consuming or daunting, so I offered the dreamers the option of a phone interview. These interviews were recorded on audio tape and later transcribed. I also phoned several of the people who sent written replies to

ask for expansion or clarification, and these interviews were also recorded and transcribed. This combined approach worked well, since some people felt they could express themselves more clearly through the spoken word, and in conversation, whereas others preferred to contemplate their exact choice of words, or felt they communicated more intimately through writing, as if they were reflecting on their lives through a personal and private journal. Two of the contributors were talented writers who adapted their unpublished material to suit the interests of this work. The overall result was a range of expression and style which complemented the variety of stories being told.

Confidentiality was a major consideration in preparing this book. All contributors were invited to choose a pen name for themselves and for other people who appeared in their dreams, and to change place names to prevent identification. All other details are accurate. Finally, after preparing the manuscript, I invited each dreamer to check and edit their story. They all did. What you read on the following pages is what actually happened, without any distorted perception from the author!

Forty-five life-changing dream stories are told in this book, twenty-six in detail, and the remaining nineteen in a series of inspirational glimpses. Each dream, combined with the actions taken by the dreamer, reflects several overlapping themes. Fifteen dreamers took action on some sort of instruction given in their dream, while fourteen dreams revealed aspects of self-understanding. Ten dreams had a highly spiritual content, while nine exhibited themes of reassurance or support. Releasing past hurt was common to eight dreams, while taking back control of a situation, precognition, realising potential, improving relationships and getting answers to important questions were each observed six times in various dream accounts.

I have chosen to present the dreams in six central themes — Spirituality, Following Instructions, Releasing the Past, Precognition, Realising Potential and Seeking Answers — simply because these represented a wide cross-section of the themes present in the dreams. Most dreams belong in several categories, and I could have elected to categorise the same dreams under completely different headings. The point was not to focus on labelling, but to compare how different dreamers handled similar themes. My research findings based on these comparisons are incorporated in the text.

Each story begins with the life-changing dream, simply because, in each dreamer's life, the dream itself was really the start of it all. As you read each opening dream, try to experience it as the dreamer might have done; let the mystery of it wash over you, then follow the dreamer's footsteps to discover how each dream translated into life-changing consequences. After each story I have added 'Jane's Interpretation', to help guide you further in your understanding of dreams and how to make practical use of them. These sections throw added emphasis on the original interpretations, or suggest parallel meanings which the dreamer may have missed. I have also included useful techniques and hints on elucidating dreams, using these dreams as examples. You will find strange and beautiful dreams, but you will also find some which run close to your own dream experiences. My interpretations, suggestions and ideas, combined with the inspirational tales told by the dreamers, should give you all you need to embark on your own life-changing adventure.

But wait one moment: before diving into the rivers and dipping into the ocean ebbing and flowing through the rest of this book, I'll give you some advance preparation skills.

# How to Make Your Dreams Truly Life Changing

What kind of dream does it take to change a life? A number of the following life-changing dreams were exceptional, once-in-a-lifetime experiences, but many started out as 'just dreams', of the kind we toss and turn over each night. We often forget that each and every dream holds transformative power if only we take the time to prise open its shell and find the pearl nestled within. The beauty of the pearl is apparent only in the light of day, its iridescent colour reduced to nothing but a functional blackness if left undiscovered.

Our dreams take the basic material of our lives and spin magical stories around it, producing pearls of wisdom from our errors, self-knowledge from our experiences, and beauty and value from our handling of life's abrasions. The result, though, is nothing less than a smooth cover-up if we do not recall the dreams, or do not make the effort to bring their treasure up from the subconscious ocean and into the sunlight of our conscious day.

Seeking out the pearl in every dream, no matter how tiny and seemingly insignificant, eventually builds an accumulated wealth of valuable information which can be effectively used to trade ourselves out of one situation and into a better one.

Dreams, therefore, once understood and acted upon, may ultimately change our lives. This can be achieved through a series of small steps, such as gradual changes in attitude and perception or cautious actions in the waking world; or might come as mega-powerful, almighty milestones complete with clear directions to get us to the next destination on our personal journeys. Either way, a dream is 'just a dream' unless our faith in it is strong enough either to take action or to allow it to lead us. That is one thing which all the life-changed dreamers in this book shared: faith in the importance and relevance of their dream to their waking life.

So how can you make your dreams truly life changing?

Firstly, don't sit and wait for the big one. Start recording every dream in a Dream Journal, alongside a brief diary of your waking thoughts, emotions and the daily challenges or triumphs of your life. Over a period of time you will come to see patterns between your daytime experiences and your dreams. You may see aspects of events and feelings from the day before being considered in your dream. Or you may see learning or synchronicities from your dream unfolding for your reconsideration in the days which follow. Undoubtedly, self-observation is a major key to unlocking the meaning of your dreams.

Back up your growing understanding and fluency in dream language by reading about the subject. Dreams usually run much deeper than their apparent meaning, and the people in your dreams have an uncanny way of representing not themselves, as you might think, but aspects of your own personality. This deeper insight, though tricky to tap in to at first, is well worth the mind-bending, and often contains huge transformative potential. My first book, *Sleep On It and Change Your Life,* includes practical information on how to interpret your dreams and use this knowledge in the context of your waking life.

Always remember the golden rule of dream interpretation: 'The Dreamer's Dream'. People may help you on your way to uncovering the meaning of your dream, and their accuracy may or may not be good, but the last word is yours. If it feels right, if it has a certain gut reaction resonance, it is correct. If not, work on it yourself until bells ring clearly.

Weigh the voice of your dreams against the voice of your conscious world, until you see the best way to use each new perspective. As you gain confidence in your ability to meld dream insight into your waking life, start by cautiously testing the water. If your actions are appropriate and your dream ears are open, later dreams will confirm your progress and offer you the next step. If your actions were inappropriate, further dreams will inform you in no uncertain terms! The system is fairly foolproof if you measure your steps and look for feedback. As you become accustomed to tuning into your dreams and seeing the resulting improvements in your life, you will find you can speed up the action, regularly translating dreaming insight into daily choices which rapidly enhance or change your life.

We may go about our lives knowing we want change yet being unable to be more precise. If you have specific questions to address, however, you may find it helpful to take these into your dream state, as several of the dreamers in this book did, gaining successful life-changing answers in return.

The following guidelines are based on some of the discoveries made through preparing this work.

- Watch for decisions you find yourself making in dreams. Judge their worth by examining your accompanying emotions in the dream. How did it make you feel when you spoke your mind, chucked in your job, or decided to go ahead with a long-held plan? If your emotional reaction was positive, give it weight when you reconsider your verdict in the light of day.

- The more you can get in touch with, or hit, the 'feeling spot' in your dreams, the more you can judge your true subconscious wishes and needs. When writing down your dreams, pause after each dream action and ask yourself 'How did I feel in the dream (not now in waking life!) about this?' Then write it down as part of your dream story. For example 'I ran a red light and I felt happy and free!' gives quite a different dream understanding from 'I ran a red light and felt shocked at the danger my absent-mindedness might have led me into'.

- Value clarity and 'realness' in your dreams, and look for indicators of fulfilling more potential. How do you cover new ground in your dreams, and what are the accompanying feelings? Does anyone pass comment, criticise or encourage? How does this make you feel? Can you discover from the dream storyline what you really want

to achieve in your heart of hearts, and can you see which attitudes are holding you back?

- Follow dream instructions only after balancing their wisdom with your waking consciousness. Be inspired by your dreams and realise that they are true glimpses of who you really are, but realise also that these glimpses are often highly symbolic. If you find you are a murderer in a dream, for example, the dream is often concerned with putting an end to something in your life; it is certainly not saying that you are, subconsciously, a murderer! (Perhaps it illustrates the need to kill off an outdated attitude, or to bury the past and move on; or the dream might be showing you your tendencies to be your own worst enemy, killing off opportunities that come your way, or killing aspects of yourself that should really be nurtured. You will know the difference once you have tuned into dream interpretation.)
- Look for body/mind comments in your dreams: for example, emphasis on body parts, particularly if they are injured, painful, inadequately functional or oversized, to catch your attention. Scan your waking life body for additional body/mind information. Do you dream of feet and toes by night and keep stubbing your toes by day? What can this, a kind of synchronicity, tell you about your mental attitudes?
- Keep your senses open for waking life synchronicities. Do objects, people or phrases from last night's dream jump up at you in ways which seem too meaningful to be plain coincidence? Use such synchronicities, by observing their daytime context, to further unlock the significance of your dream. Look back at some of the life-changing stories in this book to see how various dreamers use synchronicity to their advantage.

- Examine your dreams for realisations and turning points. Frequently, on writing our dreams down, we use phrases such as 'then I realised', or 'suddenly'. These often highlight turning points in our perception or attitude. Note what happened in the dream, following the realisation. If the outcome was positive and the feeling was good, perhaps it's time to seriously consider acting on the dream insight in your waking life. If the outcome was not so good, look carefully through the dream to see what you can learn from this.
- Read and re-read the stories here for added inspiration, and have faith that your dreams are meaningful and potentially transformative. Not blind faith perhaps, but faith that dream insight, approached with reverence, adds a dimension of choice to our waking life by blessing us with a perception of our greater being, our true reality.

# The Questionnaire

1. What was the main dream that signalled the turning point in your life? Please outline the dream.
2 Briefly describe your life situation before the dream.
3. Briefly describe the steps you took to turn your life around, or make some big changes following this dream.
4. Looking back, how do you feel about the steps you have taken and the decisions you have made because of this dream? (Including any regrets.)
5. Was this change the result of one dream, or of a series of dreams?
6. Did this life-changing dream start out as a recurring dream, or was it a 'one off'?
7. What was the time gap between having your dream and making the changes to your life?
8. Outline your interpretation of your dream.
9. Did anyone help you with your interpretation of this dream? If yes, who? (Relation, friend, dream interpreter, psychologist.)
10. How long ago was your dream?
11. Why did this dream have so much impact on you? For example, what really stood out in the dream and why did it affect you so much?
12. Did you notice any changes in your health, or did you have any accidents (body or car!), physical difficulties or body stresses around the time of this dream? Please describe, including whether you experienced these changes before, during or after the dream.

# On Spirituality,
## Universal Life Force & God

*The whole experience almost demands a host of angels,*
*but there were none.*
LORNA

*It's as if I've been touched by some kind of energy that's*
*still here with me.*
FRANCOISE

*I was convinced beyond doubt for the first time in my life that there*
*is a creative force out there in the universe that oversees the*
*happenings here on this planet.*
GRACE

I was asked recently whether I had ever had the opportunity to talk to people who were close to death about their dreams. On reflection, I have spoken with survivors of a near-death experience or critical illness and with relatives who were aware of some of the dreams experienced by their closest kin as they departed this life.

When we are battling illness, it seems, we often experience dreams of conflict and war, perhaps as an indication of the battle within the body between the infection or cancer and our bodily defences. On a deeper level, no doubt, such dreams are perfect metaphors, indicating how we have succumbed to invasion and encouraging us to fight back. One young girl, who went to bed apparently quite healthy, became sick during the night, was rushed to hospital and died within a few hours. She was diagnosed as having a 'mysterious virus'. Her mother told me that her daughter was concerned about two or three dreams that she had experienced in the week prior to her death. These involved UFOs which seemed to be beckoning her, or threatening to abduct her. I wondered afterwards whether what this girl perceived as 'alien visitors' in her dreams were actually symbolic of the alien visitors (viruses) in her body.

Closer to the moment of death, we are often told, our dreams and visions become more spiritually charged and uplifting. In this survey of life-changing dreams I was honoured to receive the experiences of three people whose dreams at or near death enabled them to touch a spiritual energy which inspired in them all a will to live and recover.

## River 1

## Nellie – Given New Life 1985

Unaware of anything except the fact that I was dying, I waited for the moment. My physical strength had gone already, and now my 'life-strength' was ebbing away as if it was evaporating. I could see nothing, hear nothing, yet all this seemed normal. I was in a passive state: no fears or any particular feelings, just waiting and experiencing the beginnings of a process. Although it was what we call 'death', what was happening seemed to be much more than could be expressed in a word or two.

Then I detected a presence and noticed light had filled space. Instantly I knew this was Jesus. Although he used no words, he seemed to question, and it was my own thoughts that I heard

> answering, 'I want to die'. The rest of the communication was more of a meeting of my presence with his. Time had no relevance. It was as if he experienced with me an understanding of my whole life by enveloping me...my whole life, yet it may have been all in a few seconds.
>
> The only words I heard him say were given to me. He said, 'I WANT TO LIVE'. As these words entered me, they became a part of me, well and truly mine, and I answered with a new sort of joy, 'Yes! I want to live'. Then the tide of the flow of my life-strength turned. (Instead of leaving me, I was receiving it.)
>
> Then I was aware that I was back in bed (where I had been all along...at least physically anyway).

Before the dream I had been admitted to hospital. I knew I was in a bad way because I had overdosed on laxatives and couldn't stop vomiting. I was badly dehydrated and my electrolytes were all out of balance. My body couldn't take any more abuse. Anorexic tendencies had blown out all sense of proportion, so much so that I just wanted to die. Therefore I hadn't called anyone when I was sick. But two Christian ladies found me, took me to their home, and then decided to take me to hospital.

Later I was told by a pastor friend that I had been put in a room by myself to die, and that he was in the room praying for me at that time. I didn't know who came and went, as I was oblivious to everything except my dream, which was the most real thing to me. I wasn't on any drugs.

Nellie's anorexia probably started in her teens, some ten years previously, but she was bulimic for about five years before landing in hospital ready to die. During that time she worked as a trainee nurse, but was unable to hold down a job for very long. She had managed one year of night duty, but only with a lot of stopping and starting, then flunked her nursing course because she was considered too immature.

As a patient, Nellie relied on the hospital to blot out her feelings of insecurity. She didn't have to worry about looking after herself or about doing anything much at all. She had been molested and abused as a child and was constantly told that she was dumb and stupid.

Once, when I was a kid, my father got me to hold up the motorbike while he took off the front wheel. It was taking all my strength to hold it up, so I was shaking with the effort. I couldn't hold it any more. When I dropped it I was a stupid dumb female who couldn't do anything.

The psychologist who later worked with Nellie said she was close to having a split personality.

Nellie's understanding of her dream experience was clear.

I was dying. Jesus came to me. My will changed from dying to living. It's possible that the little girl in me, who had been abused, bashed and threatened, had caused the conscious 'me' to lose touch with the will to live, and that this encounter got me back in touch with wanting to live again.

When I woke up I had a new determination within me. I battled to get well. I could only suck oranges and eat dry bread for three weeks. Gradually I managed to sit up in a chair for short periods, then walk. Next I sought out a therapist who had success with bulimic patients and went on a program for several months. It started off with eating breakfast once a week and developing special habits to cope with eating. At first I couldn't imagine eating three meals a day, but yes, I got there. I still stick to some of those eating habits today. All this was just the beginning.

Nellie's previous insecurity and reliance on the hospital to look after her completely turned around.

Afterwards I wanted to do things on my own. All that fear and insecurity was going. I did go back to work, and I was still lacking confidence, they said, but the nursing staff changed one month's trial into three months because they could see me growing and changing. After three months they saw that I had changed so much — I could just about run the hospital! They kept me on.

I overcame the belief that I was dumb and stupid, started study, got my TEE, entered university and am in the last year now to become a primary school teacher. (I usually get As and Bs for my assignments now, written proof that I'm not stupid!) In between this, I studied and became an interpreter of the deaf, went to Japan to teach English, had a beautiful daughter and spent a short time in Africa doing missionary work.

Nellie signed up for work in Lesotho, a country near the Orange Free State and South Africa, with 'Youth with a Mission'. Because she had nursing experience she thought she was going to be giving out medications to the other missionaries to take out into the villages, but she ended up being a missionary herself.

The work was only part-time because now missionaries are training people of their own nationality, so I went over there not only to be a missionary to pray for others, but also to train people over there to be able to go out and do what I was doing.

We went to one village and stayed there, where I ended up praying with people. One baby was sick; it had a fever and was crying. They couldn't do much for it. I had some Panadol on me and thought a quarter of one would help bring the fever down. It really needed to get to the hospital but there was no way due to distance and transport. We prayed with it and the next day someone had 'foot the way' (the local term for running the distance) all the way from his village to tell me that in the morning they got up expecting the baby to be unwell (a quarter of one Panadol would last about four hours at the most), yet it was completely well, playing with its toy in its cot.

It was while she was in Africa that Nellie discovered something that spoke louder than prayer. Training the African leaders in missionary work was exciting but demanding, and she found her first meetings with the chiefs confronting. They asked complicated questions which she felt inadequately prepared to answer.

I knew that I really needed God to give me answers. Every morning when we got up we prayed and I spent a special time in giving myself to God and seeking Him. As a result, every time we were asked questions I had an answer. For example, one chief asked 'How can God be Three in One?' and I used water, ice and water vapour to illustrate. I just felt I was standing there and it was going through me. Everyone over there wanted to hear. They'd stop me in the street. They'd run after me.

Throughout this experience, the most important learning for Nellie was this:

Although I was giving, I was receiving.

All this is the result of this one dream. Other dreams seem to be confirmation, or part of the actual sorting out, like an unfolding. By going through with this 'leading', I have come to know myself. The work that I have done for my own personality and emotional stability has given me confidence and I have an inner strength that will be with me, no matter which vocational path I choose.

The psychologist who diagnosed my fragmentary state was amazed when he worked with me, because after four years he said he didn't need to see me any more, whereas some people take a lifetime to deal with similar problems. I haven't been in hospital since. I feel that I'm living a life that's fairly normal now. Beforehand I would talk to people and there was a lot of stuff going on in my mind about not feeling good about me — I didn't feel that anyone else could feel good about me. Since this experience I've somehow got to know myself better and been able to accept that there is good in me and that other people can see it.

All this would never have happened except for the fact that the dream gave me the 'knowing' that I needed a sense of purpose. Instead of being a small me I feel the possibilities are now so wide, that as I take direction and I come towards where I feel I should be, there's more direction, more opening, like an unfolding. My aim is to finish my Bachelor of Education and then possibly do remedial work with the deaf. I also feel that I can help other people who have been through emotional turmoil, who may have a lack of success in their own life and don't feel that they're worth anything, by my life, my example. I don't feel I have to work within the church, because I think the church has got what it needs.

In the years before her death-dream experience, Nellie had been to church, but always felt like leaving because she could feel no sense of belonging. Although the dream can be credited with nothing less than restoring her will to live and saving her life through her spiritual interaction with Jesus, Nellie says she is not a Christian fanatic.

Now I don't feel I have to go to church as far as my spiritual growth and my relationship with God is concerned, but I feel that it does me good to go there, especially to join in the singing and in my worship. I find that builds me up even more than the preaching. Sometimes I'll go and listen to the preaching and something might come out and come alive to me, or sometimes I'll go into the Sunday School with my daughter because I'm getting her settled — it doesn't worry me whether I miss out or not. Praying together with someone else I find strengthening. My prayer life could weaken if I don't occasionally get with someone else and pray.

That Jesus gave His life to me, and together we made it mine, has always been a marvel to me, and I found that the Scriptures meant He not only gave life to me but gave His life for me. It all seems so real now.

## Jane's Interpretation

Nellie's dream experience undoubtedly reversed her will to die into a will to live, and has shaped her life drastically since then. Obviously on the verge of death at the time of the dream, neither I nor any other dream interpreter would have been around to offer advice which would have been heard. The dream fulfilled its purpose and, as such, needs no interpretation.

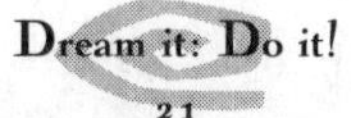

# River 2

## Dee – Reason for Being 1965

I blacked out in hospital.

The next thing I remember, I was lying in a hospital bed (a different one than my own) and I was lifting out and away from the pain. I rose through the ceiling upright and looked down through it (in reality I would have been sitting on top of another patient, as the floors and rooms were all set out the same, but I was in another dimension).

I saw my doctor down there thumping my body on the chest. There were other doctors around the bed. I saw him looking worried and he said 'We've lost her'.

Over to the right of the room near the door was a priest with his vestments on, and I assumed I had been given the last rites. Although not a practising Catholic, until then I had considered myself a Catholic. The ritual meant nothing to me. To the left of the bed a nun was praying with her beads. All of this I later verified.

I thought 'I'm dead'. It didn't bother me at all, and that surprised me. I looked around me and upwards a little to the right I could see that I was moving slowly toward a tunnel. All around me it was like space as we've seen it nowadays on TV or the movies. But we hadn't then. When I moved into the tunnel the walls appeared like see-through corrugated iron and I could see lots of confetti-like speckles of coloured lights. I felt I had my complete body and that I could put my hand through the wall of the tunnel. There was light up ahead. And I felt totally peaceful and was looking around at this new experience.

I drew up to the end of the tunnel and the light was brilliant. When someone spoke I knew it was my good friend, not from this life, and that He was there to welcome and help me. He said 'Are you ready?' I knew it was my choice and that I could go on past him to a beautiful garden with fountains. I wanted so much to go home, but I thought 'I haven't done anything yet', and I saw, or remembered (I'm not sure which) my children (my friends) as they had been before we all came into this life. They were adult figures and two of them hadn't been born to me yet. We had arranged to be together and I would have let them down. And it was the first time I would ever be a nurturing mother.

I thought, or said 'I must go back'. And I zapped down that tunnel, whoosh, and came back to the room above the bed. I saw that little had changed in all that time. I entered my body, feet first into the top of the head, and as my feet reached half way down the body I felt dreadful pain. I was crying, for it was like being born again. I heard one of the doctors say 'We've got her', and I had time to think, before blacking out 'You haven't got me, I came back'.

It was on 7 July 1965 when I first had a life-changing dream experience. I was in hospital and it was the third day after my fourth child had been born. Earlier in the afternoon I had had a very bad emotional shock which I had tried to keep to myself. At approximately 10 pm I was cleaning my teeth in the shared bathroom when all hell broke loose. I began to haemorrhage and projectile vomit all at once. I remember another woman in the bathroom screaming, then everything went black.

What makes Dee's dream experience particularly unique is that she had never heard of the tunnel or near-death experiences at the time.

It was a good five to six years later before I heard of anyone else having a similar experience.

My life situation before the 'dream' was totally chaotic and stressed. I was in a very bad marriage and all my good friends had moved away. I had had an emotionally deprived childhood and had learned little from it but to rebel. I charged into and out of every situation without thought, constantly making mistakes and blaming the world for them. I was lost.

The previous year I had a cancer biopsy of the liver and my gall bladder taken out. Two to three years earlier I had five car accidents during a twelve month period.

What struck Dee most about the dream experience was that it revealed her reason for being here. Mentally she accepted this immediately, but the physical changes took another two or three years to put into action.

I accepted for the first time that my first child, who I, as a single parent, had adopted out, hadn't chosen with me to be my nurtured child. My attitude toward my other children changed because, although they were tiny and needed to be cared for as children, as souls they were the same or near the same age as me. I waited with anticipation to have the other two children (friends) join us, even though the marriage didn't improve and my doctor had told me I wouldn't live through any more children.

I realised the importance of not wasting any learning experience in my life. I knew that patience was a huge lesson for me to work with and recalled that I must be patient with myself and others, although I have often fallen down on both. If mistakes were made, they too were learning experiences.

I have since lived with the utmost certainty that this is one of the lower dimensions, that I chose the type of life I have come into and keep projecting upon myself, and that I constantly have further choices of what I do with it. I also came back with far more psychic ability than I had before the dream.

I divorced my husband six months after my sixth child was born. It was frightening, but the 'dream' gave me strength. I was a single parent until my youngest child turned twenty-five, by which time they had all well left home and were very much on their own feet. Even though I had the choice quite a few times to change my marital state, it never seemed right. I realise now that that also had been my children's, and my own, original plan.

In May 1994, I had a similar, but more vague, experience. I had had a hysterectomy after a couple of years of ill health. I married again in 1993, and although I love my new husband very much and am very happy with him, we had extreme pressures with finance and with his children constantly causing major disruptions. The operation went very well but, a week after coming home, I again started to vomit and have diarrhoea. I was admitted to hospital but they couldn't stop the sickness. This continued for five days when I was in and out of consciousness.

> On the fifth day I came back down, for I knew I had been up there again but can't remember specifics. I remember opening my eyes and I could see the room clearly for the first time. I thought to myself 'I know what I have to do. I must help people with death and dying'.

As soon as I thought this I began to feel a little better. I stopped being sick and slowly recuperated. I would say that I definitely project myself towards these near-death experiences because I am not listening to my guides and am going the wrong way.

It took me a while to get my strength back and then I started to search, wondering what, precisely, I should be doing, rejecting this situation or that. Finally, because I thought I might be wasting time, I went to a spiritualist clairvoyant who reassured me and reminded me that I was still working with patience. 'When you are ready you will send it out to the universe and it will come to you,' she said.

So I am waiting, I hope with patience. I know a change is coming, quite soon, and that the second main work of my life is yet to come.

## Jane's Interpretation

Dee left her body at the point of death, returning later, by choice, at the moment her doctors gave themselves the full credit for reviving her. She contributed her 'near-death experience' to this book as she is aware of the lack of boundaries in defining our dreaming life. Although our dreams are most often glimpses from our subconscious, they can also encompass a wider reality, as accomplished dream travellers know well. In dreams we occupy an altered state of consciousness from which we may perceive alternate realities. Sometimes events viewed from this perspective can be later verified, as in Dee's case. On our return we may or may not use the word 'dream' to describe what we have experienced.

# River 3

## Sarras – Life: Live in Fear Every Day or Live in Faith Every Day 1992

I went to a hospital to visit a man I knew. When I got there, he was not in his bed, but his belongings were scattered all over the floor. I was down on my hands and knees trying to pick everything up. I looked up and over to the next bed and there was this huge, massive white chook.

I was scared at first, then I noticed its eyes. They were jet black and so full of love and tenderness that I was just going into this feeling. As I felt this love, the feathers all melted away and the chook disappeared, and in its place was the most beautiful face I have ever seen. It was full of love, peace and tenderness. It was very spiritual. I just wanted to stay there in that love.

I was a mess. I had sole responsibility of my mother who had dementia and was having a series of small strokes. The dream was in May and she died in July. I was also going through a very difficult separation from a guy who was threatening to kill me and following me, and I was having a hormonal problem during menopause.

Although the dream had great impact, it took two more months and a series of crises — including losing her job because her ex-lover turned up at her workplace and threatened to shoot people, the death of her mother and subsequent feelings of loneliness and guilt, her nervous breakdown and, finally, a suicide plan that almost succeeded — before the true force of the dream stepped in at the crucial moment to turn Sarras's life around.

The guy I was separating from (and who was the character in my dream) was a real Rambo sort of person. He had about 90 guns and also rifles. I didn't realise until later that there were loaded rifles in the wardrobe. One night he had one out and was threatening to shoot me. He had bows and arrows and numchuckers: he was a Karate fellow into violence. When I wanted him to go and he wouldn't, I said I was going to get the police. He said 'If you bring the police in, I'll take as much ammunition and guns as I can and I'll take as many with me as I can'. You see, you don't know. I'd spoken to the police and they said it's up to you, you know him better than anybody, which way he'll go, but I honestly didn't know.

I had been looking after Mum for about two years by the time she died. She was in a home nearby and I used to bring her out on weekends and go down every two days. Before she got too bad I used to take her shopping, or we'd go and sit by the river.

Before Mum died I wanted to know just exactly what was wrong with her. I thought her problems were due to her medication. She was on anti-depressants, uppers, downers, you name it! I took her to see a psychiatrist. Later I decided to go and see him. I went for about three or four visits, but felt that this form of treatment was of no benefit.

Sarras was able to appreciate the meaning of her dream, but sometimes it takes time and a number of violent reminders before we really get the full message.

I can still see that face in the dream, and feel the feeling that went with it. You know when you see a magnificent sunset or something and you just stand there in awe of it? That was the feeling of the dream. It was like looking at a spiritual picture. I am not a church person, but it was like a religious experience and a knowing that fears can be found and removed. The feeling of being surrounded by love was the start of it all.

My understanding of the dream was that I was always trying to rescue people and get their lives in order, trying to pick up bits and pieces, as in the dream. As a child I was attacked by a large rooster so I had a fear of chooks. I was scared, but when I looked into the eyes the fear fell away. It meant if I could face my fears they would go away, and it was as if I saw the face of God and felt I would be taken care of.

Months later I was introduced to different books and things: intellectually you understand something and say 'Yes, I know that', but it's not until you have the feeling that goes with it, or the actual understanding that you can do it. People can read it 'til they're blue in the face, but you need to feel it to know it. The difference is actually doing it in your life.

While Sarras can put her understanding into practise now, she still had to experience more before she had the courage to take the dream's message into her life:

All my life I didn't learn my lessons, so it was like 'We're going to give it to you all at once!' I can look back on it now and realise this.

Mum died in July. I just felt my world was finished. I was broke, Mum was dead and it was a big drama going up north for her funeral. I had to be a pall bearer and Mum and I weren't close, so I felt really guilty because I felt what I did for her over those two years was done out of duty, not out of love.

I came back from the funeral and found that I didn't have a job. Apparently while I was away my ex-lover had gone in and created a scene, threatening the manager and threatening to shoot people. I was asked to take some time out, without pay, until he settled down. I had a mortgage so I was financially strapped too.

The guy had met another lady, but he was still hounding me. When it came to the crunch I got a police protection order and he just turned to jelly, but he still used to ring at 3 am, leave messages and spy on me.

I just felt everything was gone. I was standing there one day and I had a handful of money and I couldn't work out what it was. I couldn't count it and I panicked. It was a real panic attack: you know you've got money, but how much is it? I looked up at the clock and I couldn't tell the time. It was just awful.

I went to the doctor and just burst into tears. He diagnosed maximum stress. When I went to see him the next morning he said I might have had a little stroke because one side of my face was a bit different. 'That's breakdown material', he said. I wasn't sleeping or eating: I couldn't even drink coffee. I was just existing on nothing. He started me on hormone replacement but wouldn't give me sleeping pills because, I think, of the state I was in. He gave me very mild sleeping tablets that pilots can take, but he'd only give me two at a time. I had to go in every day and get another two. He must have sensed the shape I was in, but they just weren't helping at all. It was that weekend that I considered suicide.

I had it all planned out. I was going to gas myself in the stove. It was winter and I had the wooden fireplace going. I wrote a note for the kids and thought 'This is a real cop out but I can't stand it any longer'. I was lying on the floor and was ready to do it, crying my eyes out. I went and turned the gas on and suddenly the dogs came in and then the cats. I've got this big old German Shepherd. I was sitting on the floor crying and he was stroking my face with his paw. The animals being there made me realise that the gas build-up would cause an explosion and would kill them as well. I knew I couldn't do it like this.

I was lying on the floor saying 'Please Jesus, help me'. I'm not a religious person, so I was thinking 'Where did that come from?', but I guess that's the point you get to. It's the only thing you can think of, to ask for help.

All of a sudden I remembered the beautiful face from my dream.

That was my rock bottom. I thought 'The future's got to be better, I've hit rock bottom, now it's up'. I was really proud that I'd worked it through. I already had an appointment booked with the psychiatrist for the next day, so I went in and told him what had happened, saying 'I've decided the future's going to be better. That was the lowest point of my life and now its upwards'. He replied 'Oh, not necessarily'. I honestly felt like walking out and straight into a semi-trailer, so I never went back!

I am now a totally different person. It was uphill from then on. I have a few hiccups every now and then, but I always seem to remember my dream face and can get back on track. Also I seem to be presented with a dream every now and then to keep going and reinforcing my new path.

It took me two months to put the dream into action. I started attending a meditation group and people started coming into my

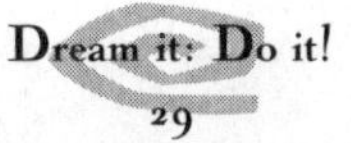

life who got me involved with others who helped me in various ways. It was like a spoke pattern, branching out. Looking back, all these caring people were on the spiritual path. Some were there for a short while and others have stayed really close friends. I feel wonderful about all the steps I've taken since then. The title of my dream was given to me by one of these wonderful people.

I've had dreams that were clearing out and reinforcing and I had some nice dreams about six months after Mum died. She had her jumper on inside out and I went and straightened her jumper out, because she was always putting her clothes on back to front and I was always sorting them out. I said 'Oh, your jumper's on back to front' and I and gave her a big hug, which is something that I had never done in real life.

No-one can believe the changes in me. I look younger physically. I used to be so thin, just strained, drained all the time. I've gone back to being a kid again. I really enjoy life now. I never enjoyed life before: everything was a drama and a big burden and struggle. Now I just have fun. I do things I would have been too scared to have done before. Going on the roller coaster, for example, and scary rides. I don't seem to have any fears of any description.

One of my biggest fears was of being on my own. I had such a low level of self-love that I only felt good when I was with someone who needed me. After the dream and the feeling of love in it, I now know that I am never alone and the inner peace of that realisation is just indescribable.

I used to be worried sick about money, but now I just think 'Something will turn up'. It always does. Any hassle that comes into my life I just say 'OK, there's no point worrying about it'. That was one of the things meditation classes instilled, that you're wasting energy by worrying about something that you can't do anything about. My new way of dealing with everything now is to 'Let-Go-Let-God'.

Up until about six months ago, my ex-lover would still ring for things, or threaten to sue me, but then one day I did a visualisation of cutting any ties that were still there. I imagined ribbons between us and I cut them all. If he rings now, I don't have any fear. The last time I spoke to him I was just normal and I haven't heard from him since then. Once my fear had gone, he drifted out. The fear was the connection that was holding him in.

Sarras came to see just how much her pattern of trying to sort things out for other people, to solve their problems for them, was holding herself, and them, back.

My dad was an alcoholic and I've always had this thing about rescuing everybody. All I wanted to do was make everything all right. I used to say if I had a magic wand I'd make everyone live happily ever after. I was married twice and both husbands had really bad hang-ups about their mothers and their rejection, so everyone was in my life at that emotional level to a certain extent, but I always thought 'I can fix them'. Even in the dream I was still trying to pick up all my ex-lover's bits and pieces, all his junk that was all over the floor, and try to get his life back in order, and that's exactly what I tried to do with all my relationships.

With the kids, when I was in a relationship with their dad and stepdad, I'd be torn, like the ham in the sandwich, trying to keep on both sides of the fence. I used to wear myself out just making sure everyone was getting what they wanted. I had my first baby at eighteen and went straight from my mother to a husband who was exactly like her, who told me when to breathe and so on. When I look at my life, it's only the last twelve months or so that I've really been an individual.

People would come to me with problems and I'd try and work them out for them. I used to get emotionally involved. I'd go to bed, unable to sleep, worrying about how I could do this, or what I could do for them. Other people's feelings and what they needed were more important than mine. It's been a big thing for me to put myself first. It's all about loving yourself. I could never come to grips with that before. I thought I liked myself pretty well, but until you come to that within yourself, you're incapable really of helping anyone else.

Now, if someone comes to me with a problem, I'll sit there and have a listen, then just say 'Well, look, this is how I see it, but what

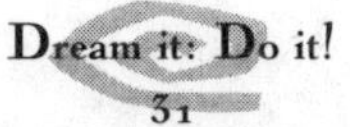

do you think about such and such, and what do you reckon?'. I try to suggest things, but it's not my trip. This is their learning process. I'm there to help, but I don't have to rescue anybody any more now.

I realise now, looking back at my journey, that no-one could do it for me. I had to do it for myself. People used to say to me about my ex-lover 'Get rid of him!', but I couldn't do it until I was ready. No-one else can really do anything for you until you come to that point in your own life.

This message seemed to be constantly reinforced for Sarras:

One of the meditation classes I attended after the dream was run by an ex-buddhist priest. He left the monastery and he has an alms bowl and just does talks. About 100 people go every week, but whatever you need is in the talk he gives that day. After a period of time, one day he gave a talk about not wanting to be a guru, that he's just there to help you and you've got to do it for yourself. He doesn't want to be a crutch, whereby you have to go every week.

I went to a hypnotherapist and ended up doing his hypnotherapy course. He said it would probably give me more benefit to do it for myself than to have it done.

Being able to see her mother and her ex-lover in a new light of perception was a major step forward in Sarras's transformation too:

Mum was a total victim sort of personality. It was a great lesson for me, having her with me, because I can see, in hindsight now, I was becoming like her. You know, you blame everyone else: 'It's their fault I'm like this'. The ex-lover was so possessive and dependent and then I realised that I had a lot of those qualities too.

I look at them now and people say, 'Oh, you must really resent that guy for what he did', and I say, 'No, I don't'. I can send him love in a meditation really genuinely and I thank him because if it hadn't have been for what had happened, I wouldn't have been where I am now.

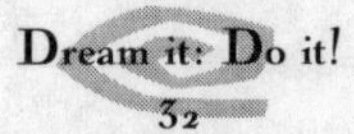

I can now feel unconditional love for everyone. I had read books about it and had talked about it, but now I am living it. My way of expressing this love is first to accept everyone for who they are, what they are and where they are coming from and not have any expectations attached to them.

## Jane's Interpretation

Sarras's dream is a parable: 'In facing fear we discover peace'.

As a child, Sarras had been attacked by a large rooster, so the massive white chook (the dream going for large-scale impact) represented fear. Fear can grow way out of proportion and it is often the case that confronting this fear and disarming it is easier than living with it. The act of gathering up the courage to face the fear is often sufficient. The feared person or event can disappear in a puff of insignificance in comparison to the strength gained through plucking up the necessary courage. In meeting our fears we come to understand ourselves and life more clearly, and in so doing, become more at peace with ourselves.

Sarras's dream revealed her tendency to pick up this man's bits and pieces (put his life together) out of fear. ('One of my biggest fears was of being on my own. I had such a low level of self-love that I only felt good when I was with someone who needed me.') The hospital setting probably represented the potential healing inherent in this insight. Taking the dream interpretation a little deeper, the man, though known to Sarras in her waking life, could be seen as her own 'inner male' who was scattered in relationship to the outer world. Sarras's outer world was in bits and pieces and she had been trying to clear it all up and make sense of it. The dream showed that her task was to face deeper fears, heal herself and move forward, rather than to concentrate on trying to put the old bits and pieces back together again. What Sarras needed to address in her inner life was playing in front of her eyes in her outer life, in her relationship with her ex-lover.

Each dreamer was asked to describe their life situation before the dream and also any particular changes in health or stress around the time of the dream. From their replies I perceived six of the forty-five dreamers to have been in a state of 'major crisis'. When I compared their dreams, I discovered that five of these people had intensely spiritual dreams (Lorna, Francoise, Nellie, Sarras and Dee). The sixth dreamer in 'major crisis' was Wraith.

Wraith was very ill, hospitalised with hepatitis at the time of her dream. While her experience is not directly spiritual in the usual sense of the word, her vision led to her decision to return to her spiritual path and evolve further. Wraith's crisis situation, it would appear, was the necessary state for the sowing of the seed.

## River 4

## Wraith – There is No Time 1966

> I was aware that I was in an asylum and something told me that it was London, or thereabouts, and it was towards the end of the 1700s I would say. I don't know why I think it was that time but that's what I felt. It was a totally bare room except for a tarpaulin on the floor. Although I knew I was considered insane, inside I didn't feel insane. I was treated like an animal. I'm really not quite sure how I died, whether I died from neglect or whatever, but as I was dying I remember saying 'I have to do something to put this right'. There was another woman with me in the cell and I recognised her as a lady with whom I'm still friendly in this life.

Wraith had been in hospital for many weeks, very ill and weak with a severe bout of hepatitis. She had been extremely stressed for a long time and was now in a situation of personal crisis. She was still in hospital when she had this dream.

The dream helped me to realise the purpose of living and it helped me to get myself into perspective. I should add that I always felt I was half awake at the time. It was certainly not a 'sleeping' dream. The experience was totally vivid, I was sort of in two bits: I was in the bed but I was also in the cell. For many years I believed it was recall of an actual experience, although I didn't know it immediately. It came to me over a period of time when things suddenly started to fit together.

Shortly after the dream, while still in hospital, Wraith was presented with a book by a visiting minister: *Elizabethan Episode* by Daisy Roberts. A message in one of the margins urged anyone interested in contacting the author to do so, and Wraith did. To her delight she found she lived nearby, and their meetings led to further contact with people and books which pointed her back to a path which she has followed over the twenty-eight years since the dream.

I have had absolutely no regrets about being led back to the path, for that is what it was. I had first begun walking it when I was very small. It also led to one of the most fulfilling experiences of my life: the establishment of a school for adults at a major psychiatric hospital. I believe I was given the chance to fulfil my vow made when I was an inmate.

When she was first married, Wraith and her husband moved out west, and she soon found herself teaching. In her class was a boy with whom she felt an instant affinity which has existed to this day. It eventuated that he was the son of the woman who was in the cell with her in the 1700s. Later, after ten years at an all girls school and becoming senior mistress, she reassessed her work:

I suddenly felt, 'I've got to change', and I was given the chance, after many knock-backs, to do this job at a major psychiatric hospital. I felt an instant affinity with people who'd been in locked wards there.

Wraith had resigned her position at the girls school and taken a lower salary to set up a school for adult inmates, because she felt that this was her chance to keep the promise she remembered from her dream back in 1966. She had to work from scratch because, although the school was a suggestion from the Department of Health, it was not backed by any government funding. She even had to find a suitable building to turn into her classroom.

There was an old disused morgue there and it was absolutely wonderful because, as soon as I said what I wanted to do, painters and carpenters offered their time for free. I went to Apex and told them that I needed money for pencils and whatever, and they supported me.

For a time the patients didn't come to the school. I had to go over to the main hospital and I had to go into locked wards with warders: these were the people I was to deal with first up. They took their clothes off, they were just like animals. After a period of about a year they were allowed to walk over to my school, in a line, with a warder.

I was teaching them all sorts of things because there were some there who were illiterate in their own language. I had a number of migrant students who were classified as schizophrenic, but now I realise that some of them were genuinely hearing another voice. I taught them basic literacy, but because they'd been in locked wards for so long that they had forgotten many things: food was just coloured blobs that came out of stainless steel containers. They'd forgotten the names of vegetables or how things grew. So we planted vegetables and we cooked them. I would eat with them. They'd only been eating with their hands before, since they weren't allowed knives and forks because they were considered dangerous weapons.

They didn't know what they looked like, as they hadn't been allowed a mirror, so I put up mirrors in the school and gave them a comb and a toothbrush each. It was incredible when they looked in them, you wouldn't believe the look on their faces. I taught the women to sew and took some of the better ones down town to shop on their government pensions and we managed to get them clothes that dignified them. Sometimes I brought the patients to my house and we ate in a normal home.

A journalist, reporting on the school at the time, wrote: 'It's when one sees these people that understanding dawns on why the institution is called a special hospital. These are sick people in need of special care. Mad? Not a bit! They are individuals who have been beset by physical or emotional disorders. Now they are convalescent, and soon they will be discharged. If the community will make room for them in its ranks.'

Wraith felt that because she had experienced being locked in inside herself (in the dream experience, in her past life, in aspects of her present life) she had reached a state in her development where she could see beyond a person's body 'doing silly things. I think the patients could sense that. Naturally you can't put it into words.'

The combination of the dream experience, her reading, the path she has followed since the dream and the teaching experiences at the psychiatric hospital has led Wraith to that point of seeing well beyond the physical existence of the body.

I've realised the total nonsense that the body is. I've learnt to look at people in a different way. In fact I've realised the non-reality of all things. I used to be very interested in reincarnation. In the dream experience I said 'I must do something about this', and repeated for many years 'In this life I was given the chance to put it right'. I realise now that it's all just a script you write yourself. We are just writing scripts until we finally learn, until we write (right) ourselves to the conclusion. It is all a dream and there is nothing but love. That is how it has totally changed my life.

A few months ago I felt I needed to write this:

I was a blank cell,
four stone walls;
I could see no window,
only the canvass covering

masking falls,
softening the yells,
the crazed crying
of the shell I thought my body.
Inside was sanity — and knowing:
I must remember this.

In the next 'life' that came
I played the game
of expiation.
I believed I must set free imprisoned bodies,
such as I had been.
I spoke to an imprisoned soul
but sought to set it whole
physically.

Then one night, reading,
suddenly I saw the prison
I remembered from my dream
was but an allegory;
the cell walls were my body,
and the dying wish, the urgency,
God's voice:
'Fret not the body
but set the Spirit free'.

## Jane's Interpretation

Wraith's experience took place when she was half awake, half asleep, so that it felt more like a vision than a 'normal' dream. If we begin our return to waking consciousness while still dreaming, and get as far as opening our eyes, we often see the dream projected onto our waking environment. This is because the brain is confused with two visual inputs (the dream and the waking surroundings). It analyses the situation then decides the two images are part of the same scene. This is why visions upon waking are not uncommon. They are known as 'hypnopompic hallucinations'. Once fully awake, the dream vision tends to fade, leaving us shaking our heads in wonder.

In the same way as we fall asleep or drift in and out of sleep, we often experience dream-like snapshot visions, like 'slide shows'. Technically these are not 'normal' dreams because they are not accompanied by REMs (the rapid eye movements which signal the physiological dream state)or by the brainwave patterns which are characteristic of physiological dreaming. This is known as 'hypnagogic' sleep. As we fall asleep we often maintain a dual awareness of our external surroundings and the hypnagogic images. The brain may present these as parallel 'realities' (as in Wraith's dual awareness), or it may rationalise the two sets of sensory data by merging them as one experience.

Wraith's experience, however, had the fluidity and emotional content of a dream, not a hypnagogic 'slide show'. If, alternatively, her vision was a hypnopompic hallucination, it was unusually long and detailed, unlike the often reported fading vision of a person or visitor from outer space.

Wraith's experience may have been a partially lucid, or near-lucid dream. In a lucid dream we are consciously aware that we are dreaming. The experience is like suddenly waking up within a dream, becoming conscious of the fact, but staying in the dream. The dream then unfolds in vivid sensuous detail which is frequently described as being 'more real' than normal waking life. In a lucid dream you realise you have the power to change the dream in any way, to experience whatever you wish. The whole dream is yours to command and enjoy, if you choose. Some lucid dreamers prefer to remain passive, letting the dream happen without conscious interference, while maintaining total awareness that they are experiencing a dream. While Wraith maintained some degree of dual consciousness and experienced the vivid reality that a lucid dream can bring, at no point did she fully awake to the realisation that this was a dream experience. Perhaps the ultimate power of the lucid dream is that it allows us direct experience of a commonly held metaphysical belief that what we perceive as our waking life is actually a dream, yet another illusion in our struggle to identify a concrete reality. Indeed, Wraith's conclusion, many years later than her original dream, is just this.

Three decades ago, at the time of the dream, Wraith felt she had glimpsed a past life, a conclusion which solidified over the years, but which then dissolved as further experiences fine-tuned her perceptions of reality. When I am asked to interpret a dream in which the dreamer finds themselves in a realistic, emotionally charged, historical setting previous to their birth date, I am always aware of the dreamer's unexpressed question: 'Was this a vision of a past life?' It is certainly easy for the dreamer to conclude that it was, and it is also easy for a dream interpreter to write off all historically staged dream scenarios as past lives. My personal belief is that we do inhabit a number of bodies, although my leaning is towards a view of occupying parallel realities, rather than successively reincarnating over a period of linear time. Of course, those who adhere to the more conventional view(!) of reincarnation and past lives may be correct. The question, as far as dream interpretation is concerned, is how to view such dreams and experiences.

To illustrate the point, take the currently contentious issue of people 'remembering' childhood trauma such as sexual abuse through techniques akin to guided visualisation, hypnotherapy, psychotherapy and so on. Some of these memories may indeed be accurate, as memory repression and denial are common survival traits. However, these techniques largely access the subconscious (and may impinge on the collective unconscious too, when, heaven forbid, the client may experience the traumas and memories of people unknown to them, living or dead), and the prime language of the subconscious is symbolism. Most dreamers have experienced violent or traumatic dreams which are very rarely literal replays of the dreamer's past or literal visions of the future. Dreaming of being tortured, for example, may be symbolic of emotional oppression in the dreamer's waking life, or of the 'self-torturing' destructive traits of the anxious, self-recriminating person. Dreams of rape may be symbolic of feeling personally violated, not in a physical sense, but in an emotional sense, or in a 'I need more personal space' sense. Dreams of sex with a stranger, a work colleague or even a member of the dreamer's family are normal experiences for many sane, respectable, well-integrated members of society. Such dreams do not necessarily reveal repressed sexual perversion or a longing for incest, but are generally symbolic of our need to integrate and grow, take on aspects of those we know (symbolised as harmonious sex), or increase our awareness of the aspects of others we are unwisely permitting into the fabric of our own personality (symbolised, perhaps, by dreams of rape, disgust or loathing for the dream sexual partner). In no way do dreams of rape, no matter how real the dreams feels, necessarily indicate repressed memories of rape. In rare instances they may, but the overwhelming significance of such images, manufactured by the subconscious, is symbolic. In the same way, any vision or situation experienced in hypnotherapy, guided visualisation or any of the regression techniques should, I believe, be subject to interpretation on a symbolic level (treating the experiences as dreams) before wholeheartedly absorbing the experience as a literal memory.

If, as Wraith now believes, our waking life is but a dream, then our whole experience, in and out of perceived sleep, in and out of hypnotherapy and allied techniques, becomes symbolic of the higher reality anyway. I agree with Wraith. I do believe we experience the world falsely, that what we perceive as our human experience is reflective of our kindergarten level of understanding reality. The symbolic language of that altered state of consciousness which we call dreaming holds the key to a greater understanding of human existence and purpose.

Extending the argument further, it would be rash to label any dream perceived as being a past life as being a true memory of a past life — or a parallel one for that matter. My working rule of thumb for dream interpretation of 'past lives', which has proved trustworthy, is as follows:

Suppose you have accessed a past life memory in a dream, and you believe that you have experienced many past lives spanning hundreds or thousands of years, millions of days and uncountable daily experiences. Then ask yourself why that particular moment of that particular past life popped up in your dream last night. The reason, if the experience was indeed a past life glimpse, is perhaps 'because it is relevant to my current situation: it has something to teach me about handling my life now, or it explains, by virtue of my past experience, the situation in which I now find myself'. If this thinking is correct, then discussing the dream experience in terms of an actual past life becomes irrelevant. It is easier, and more practical, to take the dream experience as an allegory, a metaphor, a myth with a moral to the story which helps you to negotiate your present situation. In other words, it is meaningful to interpret the 'past life' dream as a 'normal' symbolic dream which can shed light on your current life. All that may remain unsatisfied is the philosophical question of whether the experience was dream or actual memory. When I treat someone's 'past life dream' in this way and they respond to the symbolic content of the dream with recognition because it is meaningful in their present situation, then I feel the dream, and I, have served our practical purpose.

Wraith's interpretation of her dream, which I completely endorse, is clearly expressed in her poem. Its life-changing nature manifested on a practical level through the dedicated work she did within the psychiatric hospital, and on a spiritual level through the ultimate understanding of levels of perception and reality, which she learned through a combination of the dream and her quest to fulfil her dream promise.

While many of the life-changing dreams were touched with some degree of spiritual insight, I identified ten dreams as having strong spiritual content, and six of these to be outstanding in spiritual experience. They were the dreams of Lorna, Francoise, Nellie, Sarras, Dee and Grace. It is interesting to note that Grace was the only person in this survey whose highly charged spiritual dream did not come at a time of crisis in her life (not, at least, as Grace assessed it).

## River 5

## Grace – Noah's Ark 1994

My sister and I are in the kitchen preparing some dishes for visitors, including my friend, Jacquie, and my father's nieces. We are preparing some sweets from leftovers, including a trifle pudding in a large rectangular tray and another dish with fresh grapes. We place both into the fridge until the guests arrive. There is no main course.

We go outside to look up at the night sky and it is amazing! There are dots and larger circular lights floating across the sky, shooting stars, and a red star that shines bright and then just vanishes, which I figure is a UFO. Then we see some amazing configurations of lines and curves that seem mathematically significant. Some remind me of crop circles, even though they aren't the normal crop circle shapes, because they have a similar feeling. Were these messages from the heavens? Or from Gods?

As we follow these symbols with our eyes, they lead us to a series of markings in the sky that are like the hull of a large ancient ship, like a gigantic Noah's Ark in the sky! Although I am only seeing its underside, I have X-ray vision and can see its entire structure and can perceive it in three dimensions. It is a gigantic formation in the heavens.

This is an awesome feeling and, to top it off, a godlike, masculine, energetic, white light arm emerges from the hull of this vessel and reaches down towards my sister and me. This lights fills me up and charges me with the full force of its presence. I can almost hear its booming voice. This feels like it's really happening

and it's something I've never felt before. My sister and I look at each other, flabbergasted and shaken, not knowing what to do next, in fact quite afraid.

My sister turns to a TV screen where an Egyptian/Middle Eastern man is announcing something. His vibes are evil, emerging from within the TV and entering her being. I'm shocked and scared that this has happened with no warning so soon after our being surprised by the heavenly initiation. I rush towards her and do an aura cleanse of her by flicking all the negative energies off her etheric body with my hands.

Jacquie and her friends are ready to leave and we go out to say goodbye. She'll be staying with her new boyfriend and I wonder if he's American, but I think she met him in the desert back in Australia. She looks much the same, with hippie clothes and vibes. Actually I want to join them down the hill at a café that sells fresh yummy desserts and cakes. Also, my sister and her husband and baby in the pram are ready to leave, too. They have decided to stay overnight at a nearby motel because it is too noisy and crowded in this house for the baby to get enough rest. So I show Jacquie the baby and walk with them down the road a bit.

I had been living on the Gold Coast since January 1994, endeavouring to eke out a lifestyle and income that suited my personality. I was struggling to overcome some long standing health imbalances particularly associated with a familial blood and liver condition. I was also making slow progress in resolving issues around parents, childhood and my current estranged relationship with a partner of four and a half years.

In general my life was comfortable but not really peaceful or fulfilling. For the first time I was experiencing some degree of stability and contentment about my current situation instead of being preoccupied with an obsessive desire to be somewhere else in the world where I may feel better. Something was missing, though.

I have had numerous dreams in which entities in the heavens in the form of animated constellations of stars would communicate to me in sound, light, symbols and movements. I perceived these as constituting cosmically significant knowledge. This dream was different. Its impact lay in its deeply profound experiential nature in which I felt that I had actually been infused by the Light of God. I was convinced beyond doubt for the first time in my life that there is a creative force out there in the universe that oversees the happenings here on this planet. The other details at the beginning and end of the dream paled into insignificance compared to this event.

A second very experiential 'dream' combined with this one to trigger changes in my life. It was an experience of healing and transforming my being/body through space and time, spanning backwards and forwards for eons in the presence of another being.

The main step that I took following this dream occurred six weeks later when I met a woman at Bond University who offered to give me light from her hand. I was impressed by her vibes and by the fact that at last I had met someone who was obviously a 'light worker' in New Age terms who had the guts to actually say that she gave light! So I took her up on her offer and went to receive light from her shortly afterwards. She belonged to a group which originated in Japan in 1959 as a result of some 'divinely channelled inspirations' through a man. When I shared my dream with this lady, she showed me a photo on the wall of her office. Lo and behold, it was a Japanese building with its roof in the shape of Noah's Ark! In fact, she told me that the members of this group were told by God to design and build this temple in those exact specifications to enshrine the energy of God on earth.

Subtle changes in my inner and outer life since then have been caused by realisations about painful experiences in my childhood — actually *feeling* those otherwise suppressed emotions, and relating them to the constant level of anxiety and fear that I have been having, particularly in the last year and a half during which I did not feel loved and wanted by my partner. I had to deal with feelings of disgust and repulsion by the smell of cigarettes on his body, a loathing of sexual intimacy in both his home and mine, and fear of being lied to and betrayed by the one person that I had trusted and loved most and who I thought had offered the same for the past four and a half years.

These anxieties led me to consult a psychic medium who brought forth the spirit of my late maternal grandmother, who I was very close to as a child. She died in 1991 before I had the chance to ask her about events in my life from the age of three and a half to six. During those years I had lived with her while my parents were away in London. My grandmother confirmed, through the psychic, that I was sexually abused by her son. He was, and still is, a schizophrenic chain-smoker who also paid very little attention to his physical hygiene.

She also mentioned that many of these sexually abusive experiences were perceived by me as dreams, which explains to me why I used to be terrified of falling asleep as a child, even in my late primary school years. I also remember that, as a child, I used to feel really weird for having strange dreams of women being probed by metal instruments, like in an experiment or concentration camp situation. Goodness knows how a pre-school or primary school age child would be aware of such situations.

All of the above had never been mentioned to any member of my family before. That same night, I revealed it to my mother. We have since been writing to each other and I will be visiting her and my father in early 1995. This has opened up a set of family and extended family dynamics which I am yet to fully integrate and deal with. I have since also experienced a bit more love, empathy and support from and for my parents. In particular, I feel less resentful of my mother's ways of relating to my father, and have been able to perceive her as being a strong rather than weak woman within her marriage. I have also become curious about her childhood history, since sexual abuse is often a multi-generational occurrence. We will be consulting a family therapist and exploring our family tree and its patterns when I visit them in Melbourne.

There has also been much turbulence, power struggles and anger in my current relationship and a reunion/reconciliation with some friends and friends of the family since that time.

I suppose the biggest decisions made as a result of this dream were internal more than external. They included my establishing a

commitment to myself to drop any states of non-peace between myself and family members and friends with whom I had previously held much resentment. The issues of abandonment, betrayal of trust and suppression of intense emotional pain have really come forward for me to heal. These include many situations from the age of nineteen to twenty-eight in which I had felt out of control with men, and powerless to say no to their sexual advances. I felt a lack of boundaries or ability to know what was good versus what was an abusive situation. Also I was aware of a general lack of ability by my parents to be there for me emotionally or even physically. I understood this to be due to their unconscious fears for my wellbeing triggering possible guilt for not being there to protect me when I was very young.

As well as the commitment to start healing these issues, a further change was trusting more in the grace and love in universal/god forces that play a large part in my life. I even started daily thanksgiving and other prayers to consciously communicate with this newfound god-force, and a few miracles have occurred since then.

Since receiving the healing light, my general energy levels have definitely improved, along with my ability to handle stress and to give to others and enjoy life. The main physical stress throughout 1994 was constant tension in my back and, more recently, actual pain in various areas of my spine, usually in the mid-back region. The muscles on both sides of my spine are usually tense and sore. My digestion had also been temperamental for the past year and a half. About the same time that I consulted the psychic, in early October, my naturopath friend diagnosed that many of my back and digestive problems were due to a parasite in my digestive tract. Using kinesiology, the specific parasite was identified and a remedy prescribed to purge it from my body. This was a fine physical metaphor for what I was going through on other levels. Since then, my digestion has definitely improved, but I still have a tense and sore back.

Due to the remarkable synchronicities that came about as a result of the very definite symbols in the dream, I will be attending a three-day initiation seminar with the group mentioned which

transmits this 'True Light of God'. After this I will also be able to transmit this light to others.

I have also been going to a child abuse counsellor weekly for help through these times. My parents have suggested I see a psychotherapist and are willing to pay for the sessions, but I have yet to find one that I feel good about. I prefer right now to rely on my own discoveries and the support and nourishment provided by my ever-widening circle of like-minded and occasionally like-experienced friends.

POSTSCRIPT

My visit to Melbourne was a big healing time for all my family, most dramatically in the form of my mother having a tumorous piece of colon surgically removed at the same time that I was at the family therapist! On my return to the Gold Coast, I feel quite different. Having now forged a stronger link with all family members, especially Mum, I feel like it's okay now to grow up as a woman. Mum revealed to me that my Grandma had confided in her about my uncle's tendencies.

In many ways a heavy weight was lifted from me by sharing my childhood phobias with Mum and Dad and through Mum revealing some of her own lifelong fears and insecurities to me. At this point in time I am still feeling very fragile: the tender inner child which is still abandoned and hurt requires much 'TLC' and nurturing, which at times I am at a loss to offer. I notice I am slowly changing many stubborn patterns of thought and action as I become more and more conscious about their roles as defences against feeling my pain.

## Jane's Interpretation

Grace's dream opens as she is preparing trifle, but no main course. Grace probably felt, around the time of this dream, that she was involved in the 'trifles' of daily existence, neither contributing to, nor being nurtured by, a more substantially fulfilling 'main course' life. Perhaps she lacked a 'main course' (main direction) and tried to make up for it with short-lived treats (sweet desserts). In the dream, Grace is preparing the food for her friend, Jacquie. When Jacquie appears in Grace's dream, she is there to represent an aspect of Grace. In other words, Grace feeds and fuels the 'Jacquie-like' part of herself with trifling matters and details.

In complete contrast to her involvement with life's trifles, she then walks outside to view the night sky and touches upon the vastness of life: the main course she lacks, perhaps? She sees a greater significance and pattern to life (symbolised by the mathematically significant star patterns). The UFO probably represents untouched, mysterious parts of herself and her universe, as yet 'unidentified' and seemingly out of reach. Indeed, she wonders whether these are messages from the heavens or from gods. Grace now sees the possibilities for main course purpose and sustenance: a greater meaning to life rather than mere trifles. Perched on the edge, facing the great mystery, what will she discover? Her greater self? God? Extra-terrestrial intelligence? So far in the dream she perceives only the fact that there is a greater significance to life and that it is time for her to explore this more fully. Whatever it is, it is truly gigantic and, as symbolised by the story of Noah's Ark, it has the power to ensure self-survival and the promise of a new world: sunshine, peace and survival of the species after the rain and flood.

Until this dream, Grace's interest in the cosmos had been on an intellectual level, even within her previous dreams, where she would objectively view cosmic patterns devoid of any associated subjective experience. This dream changed all that. Her dream of being touched by the white light of God was undoubtedly a spiritual experience reverberating at the physical, sensual level too. I believe that when we touch this spiritual reservoir we each interpret the ecstasy according to our individual notion of higher truth. We struggle for names, labels and doctrines, but we each circle the same spiritual truth. Grace returned from her dream with her own version which gave her life main course potential and purpose. For one moment in the dream, Grace was fearful of trusting herself to this new source of energy, as the TV and aura-cleanse episode shows. In encountering our greater self we must prepare to meet the good and the bad: the shadows as well as the sunshine.

With this realisation the dream closes as the characters set out on the next stage in their journey, just as Grace will continue on her waking life path. Jacquie (and the part of Grace that is Jacquie-like) is now forming a greater union (symbolised by moving in with the boyfriend). Grace feels they met in the desert. The desert represents a lack of emotional sustenance (water) as well as a generally deserted state of being. Perhaps we ultimately meet God, or our spiritual nature, through spending time in the symbolic desert, through mental, emotional or physical impoverishment. The dream baby symbolises the newborn spiritual promise which Grace will now nurture, and the dream suggests that she should find some space and peace away from the noisiness of life to do this.

## River 6

## Lorna – Harmony, Voice and Message: A Mystical Experience 1965

My mind and its awareness were present and centrally located, but there was no awareness of my physical presence, no awareness of my body at all, so it becomes really odd that I was intensely aware of colour and sound. The dream was geographically formless, with no identifiable landmarks or physical setting. There were no symbolic hills, valleys, roads, trees, animals, machines or people. There was no action at all, symbolic or otherwise. Just an awareness, mystical in power and impact, and the difficulty in explaining it except through the use of negatives, a matter of what it was not, rather than what it was.

I use the word 'amphitheatre' to explain where I was, but it was not finite in the usual sense when the image of an amphitheatre is brought to mind; yet that is what it was most nearly like. In so far as infinity can be enclosed, this was enclosed, even compressed, as if totally inside my mind. I was not grounded in any way, yet I was not adrift or floating either. I was completely without any bodily orientation. Wherever I was, my strongest awareness was of a combination of beautiful colour, light and sound. The background sound was musical yet unlike any mechanically produced music I have ever heard. The nearest I can get to an accurate description of it would be to liken it to the effect Percy Grainger sometimes strove for in his music, or the smooth sliding from one note to another that can be produced on a synthesiser. There were no clearly defined separate notes, no clear or easy certainty whether it was voice, instrument or air movement. There was no perceptible wind. I have since read of cosmic or astral harmonics. My gut feeling now is that the sound could be described as such. The effect was transcendent, complexly harmonious, soothing, peaceful and extremely subtle.

The colours surrounding me were predominantly blues, greens, violets, all shimmering, all shot through with gold and silver. Everything was sheeny, like peacock feathers, or the blue flash of a kingfisher in sunlight along a creek. In so far as there was any form at all, the bowl of the amphitheatre tended towards deeper tones of greens, rising to blues, while passing through peacock and teal and aqua tones, to rise through a 'sky' of shimmering blues through to jacaranda and violets. There were no light sources — no stars, sun or moon — yet everywhere was a golden or silvery sheen. Colour and light seemed softly yet brightly iridescent and crystalline. Despite a feeling of pulsation and an almost overpowering range of colour and light, the actual effect was, like the sound, both soothing and subtle, and constantly changing.

I have no idea how long the dream lasted but I became aware of the silvery tones of light predominating. Gradually the intensity of light changed. It was indefinable then and I still do not know how to describe it adequately. My experience of it was interior and personal rather than something wholly exterior, yet the colour, light and sound was 'out there' as distinct from something close, tangible and enveloping.

Emotionally, I was engulfed by a great sense of peace and calm. It is difficult to describe the depth of this, but it was an intensely spiritual experience, strong in itself and strengthening to me as the receiver. I am using 'receiver' very carefully, because that is what I was doing — receiving as well as observing, feeling and knowing in an all-encompassing kind of way. The whole experience almost demands a host of angels, but there were none. Nothing I have written is accurate enough to give a precise image of the experience. It was, in total, a charged or heightened experience.

The calm became almost trance-like. Almost? Perhaps trance is the best description. Once deeply into this state of stillness, calm and heightened perception, there seemed to be a change from silvery to golden light, with purplish violet-lavendery colours predominating and a change in the sound. While not exactly a fade-out, the sound of music became less central in my awareness, less insistent of my attention. At this stage I became aware of a voice, whispery at first, but becoming strong and resonant. I have no clear impression about whether this voice was male or female but it was rich, deep, melodic with a beautiful timbre. The speech was in a language I had not heard before, but I was convinced then, and still am, that it was ancient Hebrew. This may be because I come from a Judaeo-Christian family background.

I felt I understood every word spoken. I felt a promise had been made that never again would life be as difficult as it had been during the preceding months. It was only after I felt certain of this that the dream faded. The fade-out was gradual so that I was unaware of the moment the dream finally ended, but I then knew that I was fully awake. I have never been clear in my mind about whether I woke in order to dream, half woke for the duration then fully woke, woke during the dream or immediately afterwards. I felt refreshed and calm and drifted back to sleep.

I rarely remember dreams but often know that I have dreamed. Most of the dreams I have remembered have been disturbing or distressing, so this one stands out in a special category.

I had undergone traumatic changes in my life. My husband deserted us at a time when the five children and I were ill with the flu. He had planned very carefully, having previously sold off a number of our possessions so that I had been left not only without an income but also no realisable assets. Three of the five children were asthmatics, we lived in a semi-rural area with inadequate public transport, and society, at that time, did not treat deserted wives and children with any degree of compassion.

I had been forced to go to the Child Welfare Department and make the children wards of the state who were then placed in my care. In today's terms, I was receiving $2.50 per week per child and $2.35 for myself. Should I earn more than $1.90 per week, I automatically lost $2.35. Because I was not on a pension, I received no assistance with medical, chemist or train expenses.

I had gone from flu to pneumonia and the children had been told by friends' parents to keep away as our household was no longer considered decent, respectable or suitable to mix with. I could not get any form of regular pension until my husband had been gone for six months. My in-laws rejected us because we were no longer family and an embarrassment. My family were divided in attitude. Some helped where they could. Others told me I had brought shame to the family and should have worked harder at making my marriage work. Our local doctor made sure we had medical attention and did not charge for it. The milkman came from my home district and was a deeply committed, practical Christian. He made sure we had milk. Until the dream, these were the only ones to help us in any way.

Despair had been a constant. The doctor said I was too ill to even consider going out to work. I had been taking in some dressmaking before my husband left, but most of my regular customers stopped coming because I was no longer fit to know. Understandably, life seemed very bleak and negative.

To say the dream caused me to make changes that were clear-cut, objective or purposeful, is to overstate the situation. What did happen was a change of outlook. My situation was still desperate, but now I felt real hope for the first time in at least three years. Even saying that is a slight overstatement. Without other things occurring, that hope would probably have been lost quickly and I may have filed the dream differently in my memory.

As it was, the first change was that an almost stranger, a former missionary, turned up at the door the day after the dream. She brought a box of home-grown vegetables which she said were surplus to her needs. She said she had a busy day ahead and could not stay to talk, but would drop in from time to time. When I unpacked the vegetables there was a pound note (about $2) in the bottom. I felt overwhelmed.

That same day, a stranger turned up wanting some dressmaking done. A few days later, someone who had worked with my husband came by to let me know where he was living. This meant I could now take some action to get financial support and, because he was living with someone else, begin divorce proceedings, instead of waiting the mandatory two years which was the minimum at the time for a divorce for desertion. My father offered the money to enable me to engage a lawyer. I began to believe in what the dream had told me.

I have always had a religious frame of mind, although not belonging to any denomination, so it was easy to believe that I was being cared for. The fact that everyone who now began to show friendship and concern and emotional support was a practising Christian did not seem to me to be coincidental. I was deeply aware of the spiritual around me and my own spirituality. It seems natural to accept the dream as a spiritual message and I still believe it to have been a deeply spiritual experience, explicable through the noumenal rather than the phenomenal. I expect the memory of the dream to remain a valid part of my spiritual experience, a part that I can draw on again and again, provided that I live my life spiritually and, more specifically, according to what is morally right. I received an inflooding wave of compassion within the dream and I feel I have an enduring responsibility to be compassionate. The dream and my perception of its message are part of my most interior being.

The dream reassured me that I did have a place in the universe, that I was not alone and that there is something other than the visible, tangible world around us. The dream soothed me and enabled me to see my way through what lay ahead with more calm than would otherwise have been the case. The voice and the background sounds were the most beautiful I have ever heard. I have always been sensitive to colour and aware of its mood-related effects on me. The experience provided me with an anchorage from which to begin the climb back from desperation to a more optimistic and hopeful mental outlook. The dream remains a powerful, if strange, experience but strange experiences, by other's standards, are fairly normal for me.

My experience of trying to talk to others about prior events, dreams or awareness was such that I had long since stopped discussing anything inner with anyone else. It simply did not occur to me that anyone else would be interested or that I would be thought anything but half crazy or odd if I did. From time to time since, I have met those with whom I could feel safe enough to talk about it. I seem to have chosen listeners who had experiences as equally compelling or 'otherly'.

I believe the dream came in order to allow me to find the courage and strength to go on with a more positive frame of mind. The dream presaged change. It changed me rather than encouraging me to change my life through any external action. It prepared me to meet changes as they came rather than to go out and actively instigate change although, some months later, when I saw a chance to begin a small business in partnership with my sister, I felt I could take the chance. The business folded after my sister became ill. At exactly that time, I was presented with an opportunity to return to teaching. I know the dream helped me find the courage to then begin studying for my Bachelor of Arts. It had an effect on my choice of subjects and the level at which I understood and related to symbolism within my studies and its use in my writing.

Since that time, whenever life takes a serious downturn, I consciously recall, review and re-identify with the dream and become more able to cope with events. I am, in general, a person of moderate mood swings and have always lacked certainty about myself. For the first half of my life I had no consistent evidence of approval from anyone and still struggle to define for myself who and what I am. However, in my working life as a secondary teacher, in an increasingly difficult world, I won a reputation for calmness, resilience and integrity. This is, in part, the end result of a belief that nothing will ever again be as bad as at the time before the dream, that if I survived that trauma as well as I did, I can survive, or even conquer, whatever life brings. I also believe that this remains dependent on my continuing to live a moral and compassionate life.

This was the only dream which affected me consciously in this way. It remains very much an exceptional, isolated experience which, thirty years down the line, still brings comfort, calm and a sense of wonder. In so far as I was at the rock bottom of my whole life experience at the moment of the dream, it represents the most crucial turning point of my life.

## Jane's Interpretation

This beautiful dream demonstrates the sense of extreme heightened awareness that can be attained through the dream state. Not only is the dream charged with an enhanced sensual awareness, but it is also a deeply spiritual touchstone which needs no interpretation.

Do spiritual dreams come when our life is in major crisis, presenting us with a contrast to enliven our most emotionally downtrodden moments? Do they arrive when we are in drastic need of balance in our emotional lives, or of comfort in death? Are they ours in times of spiritual or religious uncertainty, or when we are truly in need of succour, guidance and a sense of life purpose? Are they merely a balancing act, created by our own psyche, yet capable of changing our lives through altered perception and renewed faith? Or are they communications from a spiritual dimension beyond our waking reality?

The opposition of dream and waking life seen in Lorna's story were noted again in Francoise's experience. Her waking life descriptions included 'hectic, stressed out, crumbling, disintegrating', while her dream contrasted this with 'touched by energy, uplifting happiness, joy, aliveness, knowing'.

Nellie moved from a life situation of 'wanting to die' to a dream feeling of 'joy'. Dee progressed from 'emotional shock, chaotic, stressed, blaming the world' to a near-death experience of 'peace'.

Sarras used the words 'mess, responsibility, threatened' to describe her pre-dream waking life, and 'scared', followed by love, peace and tenderness' in her dream.

Similar contrasts, though not as heightened, appeared in other dreamers' reports. Mell and Andy shared feelings of 'oneness' in their dreams, Susannah felt love, Heather felt comfort, and others relished basking in a life more uplifting than their waking life at the time.

If these spiritual dreams were only self-generated delusions, how would we explain the synchronicities (meaningful coincidences) which followed? To quote Lorna, 'Without other things occurring, that hope would probably have been lost quickly and I may have filed the dream differently in my memory'.

Grace and Francoise also noted synchronicities, as did all the remaining dreamers in this section.

# Ocean Dip

## John – In the Still of the Night 1968

It wasn't a dream in the sense that it was like a picture, but it was just a blackness, and out of the blackness came a voice: 'Jill is pregnant'.

I was twenty-six years old and living at home with my parents. I was working in insurance and my fiancee, Jill, was teaching in my home town. She was boarding with us. We were planning to be married in August the following year.

I awoke from my December dream protesting quite vigorously, although I knew it was right. I didn't distrust it at all. The same thing had happened some months before the dream in question. The voice was there and her period was late, but it was extraordinarily heavy and it caused her an inordinate amount of pain. I protested to God and said 'I'll never do that again', but you know what you're like when you're young! Having had that first experience, I suppose, when the second one came I didn't bother to argue.

When I told Jill about the dream she told me she missed her first period. I think it was only about a fortnight later. We went and checked it out and found that she was indeed pregnant.

I'm a slow learner but the dreams gave reassurance of God being there, and of His forgiveness, but one has to live through the results of one's own actions.

We acted straight away. We didn't have much time. The prospect of having a child while not being married, being brought up in that era when it was just not done, was a real fear. We were married in the February. I have no regrets as we were planning to get married anyway, we just brought it forward. We divorced years later, but it wasn't because of that.

This was not John's first experience of the dream voice:

I had one some time before when I was a teenager, about seventeen, I think. Again it was just black. A voice called my name three times. I knew it was God, a God who was calling. I don't know why, but sometimes you just know. Some other people would probably call it another power or something, but for me it was God and He was calling me. I really didn't know why specifically He was calling, except that I had quite some years before then, from a very young age, been aware of the presence of God in my life. Through sermons and various people he seemed to be seeking me to be one of his clergy.

It was in the early seventies, after we moved to Australia, when He put His finger on me for the last time and after a long battle I gave up, shall we say, and sought to offer myself for ordination. It was from about that point on that the relationship with my wife began to fall apart. She couldn't see herself as a clergy wife. It was one of the most painful things that's ever happened to me.

By the way, we never did tell our parents about the pregnancy, although, knowing what I know of life now, they must have been awake to us! We were married in February and my son was born in September. They kept referring to him as a miracle baby! Our daughter was born four years later.

### Jane's Interpretation

As the information presented by the dream turned out to be correct, it needed no interpretation. Who or what was the source of this dream knowledge? Was it God? Was it a feeling based on the previous experience? Was John tuned into his fiancee's subconscious mind, which would have had perfect awareness of her physiological state? These are interesting questions, but on a practical level, if you feel a dream is giving you warning information, the most sensible thing to do is to check it out, as John did.

## Ocean Dip

## Anne – My Awakening 1992

> A man, dressed all in white, but I particularly noted the long white jacket, touched me on the shoulder and said, 'Your time is coming, Anne'.

I was at the lowest I could possibly be. It was January 1992 and I still didn't have a teaching job. I had finished my degree over a year before, but there were just no jobs.

I was back being a secretary and I had a love/hate relationship with my job. It became more difficult because Andrew couldn't handle the overtime I had to do. Our relationship was sliding downhill real fast. I felt our life had to revolve around Andrew's needs and mine didn't matter.

The crunch came when I was lying on my bed contemplating my life. A thought came from nowhere and it frightened me terribly. My thought said 'God, if you don't do something I'll go to the devil'. As soon as the thought entered my head I freaked. I ran down to Andrew crying madly, telling him I was going crazy, going out of my mind. I was frantic. I had thought that by becoming a teacher I was doing what God had in mind for me.

I was so scared that, before I went to bed that night, I sought out the Bible! I opened the book to the Old Testament parable about the man who went out into the desert to find God's will and an angel came to him and said that God's will doesn't have to be found. (Jacob's Dream: 'Faith in God replaced devious schemes for finding God's perfect will for his life'.) For the first time in a decade I felt God spoke to me through the Bible.

That night Anne had the dream.

I awoke feeling confused, because it seemed so real, as if someone really did touch me physically. My interpretation was that Jesus was reassuring me that I was OK and that there would be a time when it was my turn. I felt that my life did have a purpose and I didn't feel so alone any more. I remember feeling calm after that dream and I knew my life would be fine and that I didn't have to worry any more. God hadn't abandoned me or rejected me for having such a 'wicked' thought. In fact, I felt embraced by that dream.

The changes to my life, as a result of that one dream and the 'message' in the Bible, were almost immediate but slow. I took the steps very slowly, integrating spirituality into my life calmly and slowly. I suppose I started a spiritual journey.

I went to church on a more regular basis and I started reading self-help and creative visualisation books. *Women Who Love Too Much* by Robyn Norwood was a major factor in my journey towards emotional health. I started counselling, firstly with Andrew for a short time, and then on my own. I changed my attitude and tried to live in the present and enjoy what I had.

At the time of the dream I had back pain and chronic problems with my reproductive system. Within three months of the dream my health was in better order with the help of a naturopath.

Looking back I feel wonderful about what happened. I regret that Andrew couldn't handle the changes and that we couldn't work things through together. I became more assertive and wanted, and got, my needs met, which was difficult for him to accept.

And Anne's teaching job? It came eventually!

1992 was a big learning year after my dream experience. Patience was the main lesson I learnt, while I worked for a couple of child care centres as a casual. At least I had started to work in the right area. Finally, in December 1992, I was offered a teaching position which began in January 1993.

## Jane's Interpretation

The sensation of being touched in a dream is extremely potent. We certainly experience the full range of our waking life senses in our dreams (once we become practised at good dream recall!), but being touched by a special person seems to leave a sensory imprint which lingers well into the next day. Of all the dream senses perhaps it is the sense of touching an object or a person which makes us feel the dream was real — that we were actually there.

If I was looking at Anne's dream symbolically, I would concentrate on the point of her body which received the touch: her shoulder. Shoulders in dreams tend to represent responsibility, a symbolism which we carry through into our daily language when we talk about 'shouldering responsibility' or 'a weight was lifted from my shoulders'. We mentally rid ourselves of responsibility by shrugging our shoulders, and

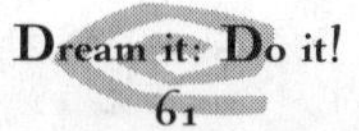

become tense and sore in the shoulder area when we feel we are bearing more than our fair share. Anne's dream, symbolically, suggested that she needed to focus on her responsibilities to achieve her just rewards. As Anne's report shows, this is exactly what she did. She took back responsibility for herself by identifying her needs and then getting them met, while releasing herself from other unnnecessary responsibilities. The figure was dressed in white, which generally suggests purity, spirituality or wholeness (being the sum of all other colours). Anne would need to reflect on what a long white jacket means to her, since this stood out in her dream. It's important to focus on individual objects that seem to jump out of a dream. Meditating on the object, writing a poem about it, constructing a list of personal associations or recreating it in art often reveals its particular symbolism to the dreamer.

Symbolism apart, Anne's dream experience was spiritually charged and gave her the strength to review and renew her life and her spirituality in the knowledge that her time would come. Was Anne touched by Jesus, or did she get 'in touch' with her spirituality as represented by the man in white? Interpreting a single vision, or a snippet of a dream, is difficult unless it is highly symbolic. I feel it is best to go with the feeling of the dream and with the message that it inspires in the dreamer.

## Ocean Dip

## Rowyn – Reality 1990-94

One woman who spoke to me claimed to be a relative of mine who had lived and died in the nineteenth century. She provided me with a date which I subsequently researched and found on the family tree.

There is no one particular dream which stands out from the rest as many have assisted in reshaping the way I live my life. Yet if I had

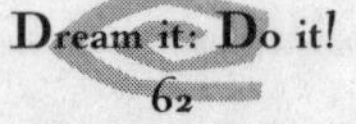

to pinpoint an example, it would be talking to people in my dream who I later find are related to my past. It is dreams like the one given here, where I can verify by fact the existence of an afterlife, that have altered my views on existence.

Years ago, when questioned on religious beliefs, I would have replied the standard 'Church of England'. Not a particularly religious person, I adopted my baptism status as a means of defining my religion. I was unaware of astral concepts and spirituality.

When my dreams started to teach rather than just entertain, or perhaps when I finally understood the messages, I began to research and self-teach in all areas of parapsychology. It was as if I were being shown the way to go, and so I followed. The moment I fully understood the direction I found an inner peace which, despite life's hassles, keeps me going.

There really has been no need to interpret such dreams. I think it's the timing in my dreams which has had most impact on me. I'm a fairly statistical person and if the information provided can be verified, I'm convinced. The changes to my life have been immediate: once I had confirmed the facts the rest simply followed.

I feel positive within myself and confident I have chosen the right path spiritually but I must confess that at times I feel as if I am leaving others behind. It's like you possess this inner knowing of how events will change or affect others but they don't 'feel' the same sensation. Sometimes it's a lonely feeling. They can't, or won't, comprehend your experiences, dreams or situation, and most of the time if you voice a dream or a feeling, they reply in ridicule and suspicion.

The last ten years have seen massive changes in all areas of my life, quite dramatic changes, most of which were far from welcome. The dreams offered an escape and I guess hope. I would hate to think that all this suffering was wasted. I like to believe that we experience good and bad for a reason and that we are meant to learn from each experience, not just suffer.

In the past I have always been an extremely athletic and competitive individual, full of vitality, and besides the odd complaint, relatively healthy. Since I began to dream, however, I am no longer the same person. I'm constantly tired, drained and suffer easily from stress. My body is failing in many areas. My hearing and sight are deteriorating, my immunity system is low, my blood is diseased and my muscles are being attacked by arthritis. Within the last four years my height has fallen from 165 cm to 158 cm. I am twenty-nine years old. Rather than challenging myself physically I am now forced to challenge mentally. I have returned to university and where once I was an average student I now succeed well in all areas of academia. It is the dreams that have brought me this far and it is the dreams which will guide me into the future.

Despite changes and challenges I do believe there is a purpose to all this madness. This is a phase, a test perhaps and one which I am determined to see through. I 'know' that I will live a long and happy life, I 'know' that it will not be alone, I 'know' that I will live in another country, write three books before I reach fifty and teach and lecture in life. I see when I dream and I feel when I am awake. Don't ask me how I know — I just do.

## Jane's Interpretation

We never know how much information we subconsciously absorb, filing away conversations overheard, perhaps even as a tiny child. At the same time, I do believe we can access information from the past through the collective unconscious, or perhaps through parallel existences or other inter-dimensional communications. Dreams such as Rowyn's beg to be followed through, researched and proved, disproved or left unproven. Such dreams may occur to educate or push the dreamer into questioning 'reality'. If, on the other hand, the information was resourced in sleep from forgotten details in the subconscious, then such dreams require more symbolic attention. The dreamer may wish to question all living relatives to build up a character picture either of the person who appeared in the dream, or of the family line they represented. These characteristics may be symbolic of aspects of the dreamer which are under consideration.

# River 7

## Cheryl – Stop Crying, I'm OK 1984

Suddenly I was sitting at a wooden table which was round, and there were four wooden chairs. I felt I was enclosed but there were no walls, just all this white light. Out of the light Leon appeared. He walked towards me and all I recall is his blue eyes. I said 'Leon, what are you doing here? You're meant to be dead.'

'I've just come to tell you I'm OK,' he replied.

'Are you sure you're alright?', I asked.

'Cheryl, I'm fine. I'm laughing whilst everyone else is crying about me.'

I still wasn't convinced. 'Are you sure?'

'Cheryl, I'm fine. As long as I'm back by the time I died I'll be OK.'

I was sort of convinced then. He sounded and looked OK and seemed determined he was OK.

With that he just vanished. I sat bolt upright in bed, looked at the clock and it was 12.05. I then spent the rest of the night well hidden under the blankets!

(Note: In waking life, Leon had died about six weeks previously, and had been pronounced dead at 12.05.)

When I was seventeen I was involved in a car accident in Queensland. Bill, the love of my life at the time, was killed: an event he'd actually told me on several occasions would happen. There was no funeral. His mother was very poor and couldn't afford to get his body sent back home. The state disposed of his body as I had no money either and all my possessions were ruined in the accident, clothes included.

I spent months regaining my health and eventually went back home to the Blue Mountains where I got my old job back and caught up with old school friends. It was good to feel safe again and back on familiar ground.

Within a span of about six months I lost at least six friends in car accidents. It was getting to the stage where I never knew who was going to be next. A guy who I'd known from school was one among many.

It was Christmas Eve and there were parties to attend. Christmas Day bore the news that Leon had been killed at 12.05 am. I was quite shocked by it. Apparently he was riding his bike and was involved in a head-on collision with a car. I was told his neck was broken. I attended his funeral and for weeks I couldn't get him out of my head. At the funeral I was so distraught I don't remember much. I couldn't understand my grief as we hadn't been that close. We got on like a house on fire but my grief seemed to go further. Was it because I'd had no grieving period for Bill when he'd died? I couldn't stop crying and every day I'd go to the cemetery and just sit by Leon's grave.

I then went on a cruise with some friends and when I got back at the end of January I picked up some photos I'd taken around Christmas. Leon's brother was in some of them and in one particular photo, which was taken at around 9 pm on Christmas Eve, an image had appeared. To me, and to others, a terrified face could be distinctly seen. The eyes and mouth were wide open, one hand was trying to cover the forehead and the other was coming up across the bottom of the face. The hands appeared large and thick, like bike gloves. I was stunned. I checked the walls, checked for grease marks, checked the angle for reflections — nothing. The night I picked the photos up I went to sleep and had the dream.

As Cheryl recounted, at the start of her story, she spent the rest of the night well hidden under the blankets after she awoke to find the time was exactly 12.05 am, being both the time of morning that Leon had been pronounced dead and the time, in the dream, he said he had to be 'back' by.

I tried hard the next day to remember exactly what colour eyes he had, but I couldn't. I'd seen him so many times but not once had I noticed the colour of his eyes. Not long after, his girlfriend came into my work with an envelope which she gave to me, saying

'These are for you'. I opened the envelope; she'd got photos of Leon done for me. I was stunned: here were the same blue eyes I'd seen in my 'dream'.

I had two or three more dreams about Leon after this. Every time I saw him he was in white light. Then the dreams stopped. Oddly enough my distress over his death stopped also.

His best friend was also killed in a bike accident not long after. Leon's mother took her own life, and his stepfather told me of things that were happening around their house that convinced him, and me, that Leon was still around.

It took me a while before I realised that Leon had actually spoken to me and that it was no dream. It would appear now that I was holding him back because of my distress. Strange things had happened when Bill had died, all of which I clearly remember, but at the time I didn't pay that much attention to them. With Leon's death I was forced to sit up and pay attention.

My encounters with Leon changed my life because I truly realised there is no death as I had perceived it.

## Good Advice 1993

> I was in a room. Three men were seated behind a desk and I was standing in front of them. I had the feeling I was in trouble. The man to my left was a guy I had known at school who died in a car accident about eight or nine years ago. He looked as I imagine he would now (about 30-35). The man in the middle was John Lennon. His hair was longer than when he died but it was him. The man to my right had dark curly hair but I have no idea who he was. They all had long coats on and Lennon wore round dark glasses and he had a file in front of him. He opened it and after reading its contents, he looked up at me in a serious but kind and loving manner and said, in his full English accent, 'Peace will come but you must be quiet!'

I had just finished reading Lennon's biography. Through my reading of all sorts of books, I had made connections with current world

events, the Bible and prophets, and I was talking to my friends quite openly about my realisations. I was also finally truly understanding Lennon's music. It was all so amazing I couldn't be quiet because I felt it was so important. I was writing a lot of poetry, which was designed to 'wake people up'. Some of it was published.

The dream wasn't just another 'dream'. It wasn't hazy: it was a definite instruction. I hope you don't think I'm mad, but it happened. It was as real as sitting here writing about it. It gave me a sense of being rapped over the knuckles and of having to pay more attention to my mouth. Its message was clear: each person realises things when they are meant to. It wasn't up to me to tell everyone, so I decided I had to keep quiet.

Anyway, I listened to the dream and I kept my own counsel a lot more. I decided not to say anything unless I was asked and I have felt good about the change.

I did tell my daughter, Kathleen, who was four at the time, about the dream. 'Yeah', she said knowingly 'They're the three wise men'. Well, it was Christmas!

## Jane's Interpretation

People respond in different ways to dreams of the recently departed returning with special personal messages. Some, like Cheryl, spend time in the dream cross-questioning the messenger, remembering that they have died and often being confused as to how they can apparently be alive again. Others enjoy being reunited with a loved one and are devastated on waking to remember that they actually died some time ago. Cheryl's reaction to noticing the correspondence of the time of death mentioned in the dream to the time on her alarm clock caused a fear/shock reaction that is often a natural consequence of this kind of dream experience.

I believe that we dream of those who have died for a number of reasons. Some are dreams in which the dreamer is coming to terms with the death, the loss of a loved one, facing unresolved business with them, or generally working out their understanding of life and death.

We can learn to cultivate or 'induce' dreams of being with those we have lost, or with those we are still grieving for, to enjoy togetherness and bathe in the peace and comfort of the dream reunion. We can bring the departed into our dreams to express farewells in a realistic setting, to forgive, to extend love, to thank and so on. Many people have perfected the art of dreaming of a deceased partner specifically to ask their advice on a matter. In many of these instances, we are making peace within ourselves, consulting the memory of our loved ones, or extrapolating our memory of the relationship as if it were continuing, taking it forward so that we can heal, build and progress beyond the point where death interrupted the relationship. Some might suggest the dreamers are being escapist, or lingering in the past, but I feel strongly that continuing a relationship after death through dreams is a natural part of the grieving process and should not be denied. When the time is right, the dreamer will move on.

Those who have died may appear in our dreams to symbolise an aspect of ourselves in exactly the same way as do people from our present life or those from long ago. The fact that they are deceased is mere detail.

Cheryl's dream, I feel, is in a different category from the above. Dreams are an altered state of consciousness, and while we may spend most of our dream time wandering about sampling the views of our subconscious in order to improve our emotional and psychological wellbeing, we also have the ability to become conscious of other dimensions. We can march across time, see the future, make contact with other people in present time (telepathy), share dreams, tune into what someone else is doing while we are dreaming (with an ability to prove accuracy afterwards by comparing notes), and we can communicate with the deceased, as I believe Cheryl has done.

In Cheryl's dream she perceived herself as 'feeling enclosed but with no walls', just as we may feel enclosed in our physical body until we realise that there are no walls: that we

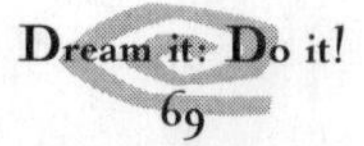

can cross barriers and communicate with the deceased because the barriers don't really exist in the first place.

Cheryl awoke to see the time on her alarm clock matched the time of Leon's death. I have seen many dreams in which people know the time and then awaken to find the same time on their clock. I believe we do have an 'eye' on time while we sleep, and this clock-sense can impinge into our dream awareness.

Cheryl's dream visitor brought life-changing material, as she expresses in her story. There are cases where the information brought by the deceased through a dream was previously unknown by the dreamer and later verified. A commonly documented experience is to dream of someone coming to say 'goodbye', wake up and check the time on the clock, and then to discover the following day that the person did indeed die at that exact time (often unexpectedly).

Undoubtedly we can and do communicate with the deceased through our dreams, but it is always worth examining such dreams for meaningful symbolism, since I suspect that the greater proportion of our dream encounters with the deceased are of the symbolic variety.

## River 8

# Violet – Dream of a Dark Night 1971

I dreamed I was watching a woman running up the next door neighbour's block of land. She was screaming. I was watching her from an aerial point of view. The scene around her was true to life, not distorted or unfamiliar in any way, however she did seem to be moving in slow motion. The dream was simply that, but it was accompanied by absolutely terrifying feelings.

I was about sixteen years old, still living at home with my parents and still going to school. To date, this is still the most frightening

dream I have ever had. It was so real and frightening that I moved my bed to the opposite end of the room away from the window, because the location of the dream was outside my bedroom window.

The strange thing was, Violet's dream seemed to trigger an unusual event which then persisted for many years.

From that time on, an eerie sound began to 'visit' me in my room at nights. It was the sound of heavy breathing coming from the window side of the room. I had not heard it or anything like it before this dream. I was so terrified at night that I put a crucifix beside my bed, and began saying the Lord's Prayer as a matter of self-defence. This seemed to work. I also had a few books on black magic and ghost stories which I threw away — and I never throw away books!

I talked the dream over with my mother, but she could offer no explanation. Neither could she hear the sound when I called her into the room. Still frightened, I brought my dog into the room, just for some moral support. I remember sitting up in bed, with the light on, looking at the dog while the dog was looking at me, a bit surprised to have been brought into my room. We were looking at each other as the sound began again. At that very instance the dog spun her head around towards the direction of the noise. This was comforting to me because at least I felt someone else could hear it, even if it was the family dog.

As months went past, I became used to this strange noise and lost my fear of it, ignoring it or asking it to go away. The noise seemed to react to my thoughts. Eventually I moved from home and the sound didn't follow me, but many years later I moved back to the old house. My boyfriend and I were in bed one night when the sound started again. He heard it straight away, and jumped out of bed to try to find out what it was.

He believed the noise to be an animal in a chimney or something. He searched and searched for the source of the noise on more than one occasion, but without success. He was so keen to locate it that I remember him getting out of bed and walking around the house in

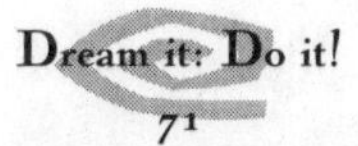

his underpants: this was something because it was winter in Tasmania at the time! Why do I think he could hear the sound, whereas others couldn't? He was a person of some sensitivity although he didn't realise it. He did say to me that as a little boy he thought everyone could see the coloured lights around people!

I believe the noise had no physical source. I think what I saw was actually happening on some level. I know the dream was connected to it but, of course, there is no evidence for any of this. It changed my life, though, because I was awoken to the very real world of 'spirit' or 'psychic' experience and began what I expect is a lifelong interest in these things.

I had always felt different from my family because they weren't really interested in any of this. I was more academic than they were, but, as time went past, my mother also became involved in learning and reading. I thought I was open to the original dream and experience because of my interest in these areas. I was dabbling around in unusual supernatural type things, and, being only young and not understanding, I was looking at the nastier side of it, the darker side, rather than the more positive.

Years later, I was married to a man who was fighting his psychic gift. It confused him so much that I decided that I didn't want to know anything about anything unless I could touch it. It was awful to see someone else get very mixed up. Years later, once I'd divorced, I realised I could go back and follow these things without anything harmful happening to me.

Nowadays I would say that there isn't anything to fear. Recently I have had a break from these things, but for about five years previously I was quite involved with meditation and other metaphysical experiences. I'd be the sort of person who would go to someone's house and see ghostly shapes. I wouldn't mention it. I was just in tune with that kind of thing.

After all these years of investigation, initiated by the dream and eerie noise experience, I feel I have processed it all and spat it out at the end. I do not wish not to have gone through it all because I feel I have learned a lot.

In conclusion my life philosophy now is that it's actually not complicated at all! There is really only one thing: just be happy.

The difference between being happy and unhappy is just basically deciding you're going to be happy. It's actually as simple as that. Simple, but not necessarily easy!

Once I realised that, I totally changed my life again. I moved out of a long relationship, changed my physical situation, changed my diet, changed my exercise program, just changed everything. It was time to work on a very physical level, to sort my physical life out. The whole experience was an education in faith and the loss of fear in conquering an unknown experience.

## Jane's Interpretation

If the dream scenery had not been so true to life I would have interpreted this dream symbolically to begin with. If the setting had been unusual or unidentifiable, I would have focused on the emotional content of the dream (terrified, screaming) and the movement of the woman (unable to escape, held back). The aerial point of view, in symbolic terms, would have denoted a degree of detachment of the dreamer, who was looking at herself and her situation, symbolised by the terrified, running woman. Although the dreamer views from an objective position, she is emotionally involved in the dream, which causes me to wonder how much more of an emotional reaction she would have had to endure if she had experienced the dream as the running woman.

Often in dreams we remove ourselves from the most sensitive episodes, or most hurtful parts, either to protect ourselves from the full emotional impact or to gain a clearer, more objective viewpoint.

In an unrecognisable dreamscape, then, this would be the dream of someone who was feeling extremely distressed, trapped and unable to escape her situation. If the dream still included the notion of the neighbour's land, the dreamer would have to think about which attitudes or personality aspects she shares with her neighbour, because she identifies with the neighbour somehow in the dream.

Even when we have a dream which is set in our present home, at work or at some other location well known to us, we usually encounter slight changes in the environment. People report dreams about familiar places with descriptions such as 'we were at work, but the office had a new window', or 'it was my daughter, but she had her hair cut', or 'we were in our house but in a different city'. Violet was certain that her dream took place in either the actual landscape of her home, or in an accurate copy of it. Flying or hovering above, or simply looking down upon an entirely familiar and accurate landscape is a dream situation which is often described as 'astral travelling'. My own definition of 'astral travelling' is quite different, and is discussed in *Sleep On It and Change Your Life.* However, this common belief does tend to set this type of dream apart from the normal 'symbolic' dream. It is for this reason that we have to look at Violet's dream from another angle.

There are many possibilities, but I believe Violet's final understanding that she was tuned into past, present, future or parallel negative occurrences was probably the case. If we can tune into others telepathically while we dream, yet also move between time dimensions in our sleep, then viewing the agony of someone else from whichever dimension becomes a possibility. If this screaming, running woman had existed sometime in the past, or in some other parallel dimension, and her emotion was so intense that it somehow imprinted or remained within the psychic landscape, then it would be easy for a sensitive dreamer to tune into.

I believe we generally resonate with situations with which we can empathise, so the symbolic interpretation should always be considered unless it does not make sense. Once Violet had tuned into this experience, it presumably became easier for her to pick up again and again, like a well worn pathway.

No dream interpretation is ever complete, and some dreams, like this one, end up more as a list of possibilities. Part of the magnetism of dream research for me is the challenge of working with an extremely difficult subject, and I feel it is better sometimes to leave an open-minded set of possibilities and offer those on a platter, rather than to arrive at an authoritative imposing conclusion just for the sake of completion. Violet, though, has been able to look back on her dream experience with more precision, since it was her experience and it has shaped her life in definite and measurable ways which have helped make her the person she is.

My personal experience is an absolute knowledge of a wider reality than the one we are accustomed to agree upon in our waking lives. As always, we live, in this life 'the dreamer's dream'. Each dream contains, therefore, the dreamer's personal truth. Each dream experience presented in *Dream it: Do it!* is for the dreamer to know and for you to discover. On one point, though, there must be unanimous agreement: these dreams, based on a meeting with the spiritual, are amongst the most profoundly life-changing dreams and experiences related in this book.

*Nothing I have written is accurate enough to give a precise image of the experience. It was, in total, a charged or heightened experience.*

LORNA

*This dream was different. It's impact lay in its deeply profound experiential nature in which I felt that I had actually been infused by the Light of God.*

GRACE

*The feeling of being surrounded by love was the start of it all.*

SARRAS

*There was light up ahead. And I felt totally peaceful and was looking around at this new experience.*

DEE

*It seems natural to accept the dream as a spiritual message and I still believe it to have been a deeply spiritual experience, explicable through the noumenal rather than the phenomenal.*

LORNA

*It was so precious to me, it was almost like a sacred passage or initiation. I know beyond a doubt that the life force, or the universal energy of life, or of spirit, whatever you want to call it, is as real as I am holding this telephone. It is there, it's everything.*

FRANCOISE

# On Following Instructions

*This dream occurred before I began to work with or understand dreams, but it was so clear and precise, so real, that I just 'knew' it was to be acted on.*

SUE

In the best of all worlds we would understand every dream, measure up the importance of its significance or message, and decide on whether action was appropriate. Action on a dream might be subtle, such as a change in attitude towards someone or something, or it might be dramatic, like packing your bags and moving into a monastery for the rest of your life! Somewhere along the line, if we comprehend the value of dreaming, we carry forward some teaching into our waking lives. How far should we go in carrying out instructions received in our dreams, and how much can doing so change our lives?

Of the forty-five dreamers in this life-changing dream survey, fifteen showed elements of following instructions received directly in the dream, either from another dream character, or from their own words of wisdom within the dream.

# Ocean Dip

## Pam – Change of Direction 1991

> I saw a set of traffic lights and they were on red. I was going to climb through some barbed wire fencing when someone said 'Go the other way'. Next there was some flooding and I was in a truck about to go through the water when again someone said 'Go the other way'.

I was having trouble working under my chief accountant at work, stressed out through trying to please him. I felt like I was getting nowhere and couldn't figure out what to do about the situation until I had the dream.

What struck Pam the most in her dream was the fact that the message was repeated. Clearly she should take action and 'Go the other way'.

Starting the next day, I completely changed the way I was dealing with him. From that moment on I seemed to go ahead in the company. Our working relationship improved, leading to promotion and more interesting tasks. I was asked to go to work in Perth for eight weeks, all expenses paid. On the weekends I became a tourist and thoroughly enjoyed my time there.

### Jane's Interpretation

The general message in Pam's dream needs little translation, but which other way should she go? ('The other way' perhaps implies the exact opposite approach to the one she had been taking.) Fortunately Pam was able to successfully work that one out for herself. In interpreting the dream, the first step is to ask the dreamer where, in their life, they feel stopped (the red light). The truck, as a dream vehicle, often symbolises work (work truck), even in white collar professions like accountancy. Floods usually suggest emotional flooding and fences tend to represent limitations. The barbed wire may have been barbed or hurtful communications between the boss and Pam. The dream suggests, then, that getting through to the boss will be most successful if Pam keeps clear of her emotions and carefully considers her words when negotiating a better working relationship.

Wraith followed her own affirmation, which resonated in her ears after her life-changing dream experience of death in a mental asylum in London in the late 1700s: 'I have to do something to put this right.' Her achievements with working with psychiatric patients became testimony to the degree with which she abided by her statement.

Calli, who was happily living in Queensland at the time and resisting any hints her husband had been making about moving interstate, heard a commanding voice in her dream: '...a hand appeared, pointing in the sky, and a voice said, "You have to move near that man over there". I turned and looked over my shoulder and there was this large man with a big head sitting cross-legged. I said, "No, I don't know him. I don't want to move!" And the voice said "It is most important that you move near the man over there".' Eventually she did move 'over there', much to her advantage as things turned out.

John shared with Calli the 'commanding voice' experience. He heard, in his dream, a voice saying 'Jill is pregnant'. Acting on this instruction, Jill took a pregnancy test, they discovered the truth of the dream, and then promptly brought their marriage forward.

Fiona's realisation that she loved Simon came in an unforgettable life-changing dream, but it received sweet backing in the form of instruction from a deceased relative in a dream: 'My dead uncle came to me in another dream and told me Simon was the right man for me and I'd better not let him go.'

Susannah took good advice from her deceased grandparents who visited her in her dreams during a particularly difficult time in her life.

# River 9

## Susannah – Meeting My Ancestor Spirit Guides 1991

My maternal grandfather, who I was very close to, and who died in 1973 when I was fourteen, came and sat down on the edge of my bed and said 'I know you're asleep but I need to talk to you'. He was a very handsome, tall man, and there he was, wearing his favourite old red plaid hunting shirt and smiling, his hair still black, his glasses and the many fillings in his teeth glinting gold in the dark. He said he knew I was going through a rough time, that I was far from home, impoverished, physically ill, lonely and that I was thinking of leaving my husband.

He said 'Don't do that. He is a fine man. You'll come out of this OK.' He said he'd lived through the Great Depression and he knew what we were going through. And I felt this rush of love and warmth, and I was a little girl again. I crawled over and sat in his lap. Then I was shocked to find myself, an adult, sitting on his lap, looking at myself in bed. I woke up then.

He came back a few more times in dreams and told me not to worry about him not being able to see my baby, because he had seen him and he thought he'd make a great kid. I always remember those words because that's just how he spoke. He'd say things like 'your hair is growin' away like a weed'. Hearing him again made me cry when I woke up.

The main dreams that signalled turning points in Susannah's life were a series she had when her first child was about six months old.

Shortly after my son was born my husband lost his job as the recession hit Australia. We had just bought our first house and we were plunged into a terrible period of our lives, with the loss of everything but the house, which we somehow managed to hang onto. I am originally from America. We were both feeling extremely stranded and isolated, having no family around to support us. I was thinking about leaving my husband, not because I didn't feel love for him, but because the situation was just about killing us both. I was quite sick physically following my first child's birth and back problems ensued. Everything possible went wrong, except for our beautiful baby boy who thrived and kept us going.

Other dreams in this series involved a woman, unknown to me at the time. She was an older woman with thick black hair, a little stooped, but very finely built, in long skirts. She'd take me walking around a construction site, where there was a big pit dug and all sorts of machines and lots of piles of materials for building, such as steel, wood and bricks. We'd peer through the fence at it.

Then she'd take me into a little white house across the street from the site. The house looked a bit like our own house, and she'd lead me down a long hall to a room painted white, where there were shelves and shelves full of bowls, all made of pottery, all painted rich shades of blue. She would tell me about them and advise me to take note of her descriptions of the bowls.

She came into my dreams three or four times during 1991 and then went away, but she came back last year, in June 1994. Suddenly, out of the blue, in June, my husband was offered a job in his profession again. He'd been doing terribly degrading jobs previously. In my dream she told me, while standing in my room, which had moved to a sort of cloud position above a long, white pebbled road, that if we put everything into the house and spent our very little cash on nothing else, we would be able to sell the house and would never be without money again.

Shortly after this dream, my parents came to visit and my Dad, for the first time, began talking about his mother, who died when he was four. And I knew that the woman spirit guide of my dreams was my paternal grandmother. I actually had a physical sensation, like in the dream, all tingling and hot all over, my heart and stomach fluttering, and I just knew it was her.

Susannah took both her grandparents' dream advice over the next two years. She started reading immediately about spirituality and psychic development, and the decisions were made to renovate, sell and move in early 1993.

Now we have nearly finished renovating our house ourselves. It has been difficult, to say the least, as we have very little money and two children now, as our second son was born in 1993. We are still in debt from the original crash we experienced. Although our relationship has taken a battering, along with our self-esteem, we're still together, and growing as people. We are about to sell our house, which, in its renovated state, has exceeded our expectations, and to move back to America to live in the mountains where I grew up. Also I've become a POTTER with a penchant for blue bowls: I am only an amateur, but I am passionate and, I think, talented!

I have always had experiences of the supernatural, but I never let myself own them or believe them. No longer! I thought I saw my grandfather's ghost a few times as a teenager but disregarded it. I've had many experiences like that since then and disregarded them too: dreams, sightings, feelings, very strange coincidences and premonitions. Now I do not disregard even the smallest thing. Since the dreams, I have been reading everything I can get my hands on regarding psychic phenomena, spirituality and so on. The last in this succession of dreams which have turned my life around were a long series of dreams last year, 1994, in which a male and female would appear and tell me repeatedly I was a witch in a past life and was meant to reclaim my power. I am now studying the Tarot in depth and looking for a Wiccan group to join and study with.

My interpretation of all three series of these dreams is that these people and guides are telling me I am blessed. I can do things, and can make it. The power is within me, shown by the blue bowls and the witches' words. My grandfather loves me and comes to see me but I must recognise my power and build upon it, as symbolised by the construction site. The general message for me has been to trust myself and go with what I want to do, to stop pushing aside my feelings and experiences. And I think my husband and my grandfather are very much alike, in retrospect.

I have given up working in my old job, as it only served to stop me from being who I want to be, and have begun, at last, to write fiction. I rely on my intuition now and trust it. My husband has come around to these things too.

I regret nothing, although sometimes I wish we'd sold the house and taken a financial loss and gone home. I think that my Grandma's advice will prevail and when we sell the house shortly, I'll be glad we stuck it out. I am pretty amazingly healthy now and have been for a long time. And even though we're not at the end of the tunnel yet, the fact is, we wouldn't be the same people we are now if we hadn't gone through this period of our lives. Neither would I be living my life with such an open mind or strong sense of wonderment.

## Jane's Interpretation

We can and do make contact with people who have passed on, in and out of our dreams. The difficulty as an outsider is knowing which dreams are true spirit contacts and which are dreams about the memory of the deceased person and what they might have said to us. Sometimes the dream itself brings information previously unknown to the dreamer, or 'proof' presents itself within a short while. The best guide is the dreamer's reaction to the 'reality' of the dream meeting. Such dreams leave the dreamer to decide whether the received information is good advice and whether to follow it, and perhaps also encourage a review of their perception of life and death.

Annie and her husband had been trying to conceive a baby for many years and had been through several unsuccessful attempts at pregnancy through the IVF program. Their one and only pregnancy during that time ended traumatically in miscarriage. Having given up and applied for adoption, Annie had a dream: 'My husband and I were sitting in the doctor's office being told we were expecting a baby in November'. She took this as an instruction to try one more time and, yes, the

dream turned out not only to bear good advice but also to have been precognitive in every detail.

Dee followed instructions which she believed had been laid down before this life. During the time in which she died in hospital, she met 'adult figures and two of them hadn't been born to me yet. We had arranged to be together and I would have let them down'. On re-entering her body and being resuscitated, Dee went on to bear two more children, despite being told by her doctor that she wouldn't survive childbirth.

Phillipa wrote a book to heal her past based on her own thoughts in a dream: 'I feel I want to write a book, starting then (present time) and going back to my childhood (the beginning)'.

Sue received a specific piece of advice in her dream.

## Ocean Dip

## Sue – Husband to Leave 1977

I was shown that my husband would meet another woman while away on a trip. I saw the whole thing down to what she looked like. I was then told that I was not to have any more children, as I could manage alone with one, and that people didn't usually mind babysitting for one, but not for more than one.

I was married to a sailor, with a baby under twelve months. We were happy and there was no sign of any problem with the relationship. This dream occurred before I began to work with or understand dreams, but it was so clear and precise, so real, that I just 'knew' it was to be acted on. I knew it meant that my husband would meet a new woman, fall in love and leave. I alone could not support more than one child and should not have any more children. I did not hesitate.

I had a tubal ligation performed as soon as it could be arranged, which was only a few weeks later, even against the wishes of my then husband.

The whole thing happened exactly as in the dream. Even the woman was identical. When the actual waking life event occurred it was rather eerie, like replaying a movie. At first he told me there was not anyone else, just that he was leaving, but I *knew* there was someone else. It turned out there was, he had met her on a trip.

Although it was three years between the dream and this event, we would have had more children in that time had it not been for the dream. Instead I was left with only one child to look after. I am glad the dream was so clear and so strong that I acted on it, even without understanding dreams. It certainly simplified my life in the years to come. I really would not have handled looking after more than one child by myself.

This was probably the first dream that had an impact on me and when the events actually happened as I dreamt them, I began to read about, and work with dreams. At first I approached them in a half-hearted way, but then with so many dreams coming, it became a very important part of my life. The move after the separation also led me into the world of spirituality, motivation, metaphysics and guides.

I have no regrets about following the dream's advice. I feel that I handled the separation much better having been forewarned. Knowing it was destined made it easier.

## Jane's Interpretation

Sue's resolve about the reality of this message was so clear that I would never have been asked for an interpretation. If it was felt to be a 'normal' symbolic dream, I would have suggested that Sue's male side (Yang: relationship with her outer world) was getting itchy feet, that she was not entirely satisfied with her present situation as mother of a small child, and that she would ultimately step away from creative motherhood to form a different creative relationship with the world. In this sense, Sue's choice to restrict her family to one child was sensible, allowing her the future freedom, in or out of a relationship with her then-husband, to express her creativity in a different way.

These and other dreamers on the survey seemed to have nothing in common other than that they followed instructions in their dreams to some extent and changed their lives in the process. Stress or crisis did not appear to play a part in their willingness to take advice directly from a dream. All believed they were acting from a measured consideration of the dream advice and were apparently confident in the steps they took as well as satisfied with the outcome.

In my own life I have tossed away many instructions heard in my dreams because I have realised they were not literal. I have been able to comprehend their symbolic meaning and put that into action instead. I don't doubt that these dreamers acted only out of certainty too.

I had a dream several years ago, when life seemed to be dealing me a few perverse blows. For a while it seemed the harder I tried to achieve my goals, the proverbial brick wall would appear in front of me. Then I dreamed I was faced with a brick house and I was trying to gain entry through the side wall. Again and again I tried, perhaps perceiving that this was a dream, and thinking that somehow, surely, I should be able to walk through this wall. I heard a strong, male voice from the sky. It appeared to come from behind a cloud over my right shoulder and boomed 'Jane, why are you trying to walk through a brick wall when the front door is wide open?' Sure enough, when I walked to the front of the house I could see a big, wide-open door, through which I walked with ease.

On waking I decided it would be crazy to turn away from every goal and walk through every open door, but my dream voice certainly had a point. I decided to follow the dream instruction for a period of three weeks only. I guess I made a pact with the voice. It was like saying 'I won't give everything up, after all, I've worked hard to get this far, but I'll give it a go and trust you to protect me as I walk through the doors'. In those weeks, among many important opportunities that came my way, I met my husband, Glenn, simply by walking through one of those doors. Had I not met him, I probably wouldn't have started writing books on dreams…among other things!

# On Releasing The Past

*'Well, this is as far as I go', he declares. Looking pensive, he adds 'I've been accused of holding you back. So, now it's up to you!' I remember all the arguments and fights we used to have whenever I tried to follow either an artistic or academic course, and realise that this is his awkward way of saying 'Go with my blessing'.*

LEE

*I believe I was given the chance to fulfil my vow made when I was an inmate.*

WRAITH

*This dream was the turning point. I interpreted it as meaning that my father had instilled so much fear in me as a child that I was still letting this control my life as an adult...It was time for me to take control of my destiny. I acted on the dream immediately and my life path has been straight and onward forward since.*

MICHAELA

One of the most powerful ways of accelerating positive change in your life is to release yourself from the effects of negativity from your past. We are frequently our own worst enemies, shackling ourselves, hands and feet, with regrets about the past, feelings of guilt, unresolved conflicts from old and current relationships, outdated expectations and inappropriate programming stemming back to our earlier years. Resolving unfinished business or making amends with the past is ideal, but the ability to free ourselves from our burdens, to simply put down the old baggage and walk away when no other approach is possible, can work miracles. Releasing the past opens up the future, with barely a bead of sweat required to walk the new road.

Dreams which give us the tools to let go of the past, if acted upon, have huge life-changing potential. Eight of the survey dreamers contributed dreams with strong past-releasing aspects: Calli, Barney, Michaela, Phillipa, Moni, Andy, Cheryl and Grace.

## River 10

## Calli – The Scarecrow 1989 (a recurring dream)

The scarecrow would come and sit on the end of my bed to protect me from dreams of the past which I didn't want to look at.

## The Game of Illusion 1990

I dreamt my husband and I were picnicking. We were sitting on a rug with food in front of us. I knew it was in the countryside, but when I looked around we were on a snakes and ladders board. The roads were the ladders, the rivers were the snakes and the trees were made of cardboard. I was looking at this scene when a hand appeared, pointing in the sky, and a voice said 'You have to move near that man over there'. I turned and looked over my shoulder and there was this large man with a big head sitting cross-legged. I said 'No I don't know him. I don't want to move!' And the voice said 'It's most important that you move near the man over there'.

Calli welcomed the scarecrow who repeatedly sat on the end of her bed in her dreams, protecting her from dreaming about her past. She knew issues needed clearing but had felt that she would not be able to devote the necessary time and emotional energy until her children had grown up and left home. That time was drawing near, and the scarecrow's days were numbered, when Calli's husband's mother was dying. Calli had never had a chance to say goodbye to her own mother, who had died when she was five, and her mother-in-law's illness brought this sadness clearly into focus. During a consultation with a visiting psychic, Calli was advised 'Go home and write a letter to your mother and your father, as you would as a child'.

It was in writing these letters that Calli realised how deeply her past had affected her, and she decided to examine her fears through a series of paintings which she began the next day. In doing this, she suddenly made the connection with the scarecrow dream: these were the fears her scarecrow had kept at bay, until now. Now it was time to face the past and clear it.

I was five when my Mum died of complications after an appendicitis operation. The family never acknowledged to me that Mum had died. I knew she was dead the next day, because I can remember being in the park with my sister and it must have been very early in the day, early in the English summer, and these workmen said to my sister 'Why are you up so early?' and she said 'Well, my mother died'. And I looked up at her and I said 'What?'. And she said 'Oh, the rabbit died'. And I'm standing there looking and thinking 'We haven't got a rabbit'. But other than that it wasn't mentioned, ever.

I was never allowed to grieve for my mother because my Dad remarried very quickly, six months later. My mother was never mentioned and we had no photos of her.

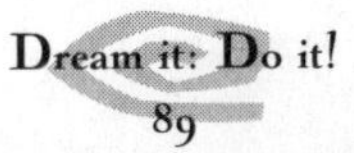

## The Letters: 1989

Monday

Dear Mammy,

I am writing this to ask why you went away when I needed you very much. Daddy said you were coming home on Thursday and you'd be here for my birthday party. But you went away and I didn't see you again and they said I could go and see you that day and wave to you through the window. Nobody would tell me where you had gone. Nobody wanted to talk to me. I felt very frightened and nobody knew how I felt. They thought I was too small. They all thought Ann was old enough to know. Nobody would talk to me. I wanted to come and sing hymns for you but they wouldn't let me.

I never knew where you went. It was like a big hole came and swallowed you up and I was frightened all the time Daddy would go through the same hole. I could not understand why you could not hear me when I called for you. If you went to Jesus like they said, why wouldn't he let you hear me and then he would have let you come back after the rest you needed. I didn't like our house any more. When Mrs Moody came things were awful and I wanted to run away to Nanna's. Daddy said I couldn't go, and got upset, so I didn't say it any more. I felt very angry that nobody cared.

Then Mummy arrived, big fires but no warmth. I needed you and you left me. I can now see you had to go and I accept that you loved me and I love you and although you have gone you have a place in my heart which is always there. I accept your departure and the love you still have for me which will go on forever. I know I will see you again and it will be as though you never left.

I love you very much and take you back into my heart as my own dear Mother. Until we meet again.

I am always your loving daughter,

Calli

Monday

Dear Dad,

This is to clear away the misunderstanding which seemed to happen when I was twelve. I still don't know why I changed in your eyes. I was still the same even if my body grew up. I was still your little girl inside. You never left into the big black hole, but you did take your love away and it made a big black hole for me. I was made to feel bad when I knew I was good. I could not understand how you could change so much towards me. One day I was your little girl, the next day I was someone to shout at and chastise for everything I did and didn't do.

I think a lot of things were planted in your head by Mum and you could never feel the same again. I know how, although you are trapped within your empty shell, you now know the truth about yourself and me. It's too late to say anything but I am safe in the knowledge that you know and are at peace with yourself and your world. I never stopped loving you although I felt so hurt for so long.

That has healed now. We are joined as we were father and daughter who were very close. I love you and know you love me. All past differences are forgotten. We are as we always were. I wait to see you again with Mammy safe in the knowledge that your love has never changed.

I will see you again, back to my Dad, and I will tell you these things.

I am your loving daughter,

Calli

(These two letters have had a wider circle of influence, since they have been used in palliative care lectures since 1989.)

## The Painting: 1989

I didn't think about what I was drawing, just as I didn't think about what I wrote in the letters. I just wrote and then I read it afterwards. I drew all these peculiar things that were saying goodbye to myself as a child, saying goodbye to Mum through a hospital window, being blown off the edge of a cliff, failing, all these things that frightened me. Then I tore them all up and made a collage of it and stuck the scarecrow on top. I deliberately put the scarecrow on top. That put an end to the scarecrow dreams and put to rest a lot of the things I was frightened of, but I didn't grieve properly until I moved to New South Wales and went to a counsellor there.

Calli's understanding of her recurring scarecrow dream deepened when a Flying Arts tutor came up to northern Queensland, when she had virtually finished the painting.

The Flying Arts were run by the Queensland Art Gallery who sent tutors to people who were classed as 'bush people'. They used to come up by plane and do three-day courses. My tutor asked if I realised that the scarecrow was the sign of the cross. I hadn't even thought of that. I went home and thought well, maybe I am being protected, because before that I wasn't ready to look at the dreams. The scarecrow was telling me he had protected me but now that my family had grown up it was time to start putting my own past to right. I couldn't have done it while the children were growing up. With four children I didn't have enough stamina. My only regrets now, looking back, are that I received no help with my grieving, psychologically or emotionally, between the ages of fourteen and seventeen. I got married at eighteen and had my first child by nineteen.

Calli's painting, 'The Scarecrow' was subsequently exhibited at the Queensland Art Gallery. While understanding and acting on the scarecrow recurring dreams brought Calli face to face with some of her deepest fears, it took a move to New South Wales and a further change in lifestyle before the grieving process for her mother was finally completed. This change was heralded by 'The Game of Illusion' dream.

Calli created a painting from 'The Game of Illusion', clearly capturing the light around the oversized, cross-legged man. Everything in the dream and in her painting pointed towards a move, but Calli initially held back. She had become involved with the local community and was secretary of the Artist's Club. She was happy with her art and painting, and although her husband had itchy feet and was eyeing up new job opportunities further afield, Calli kept reiterating 'I'm not moving. I've had enough this time'. Shortly after she finished her painting, he returned from a job interview in New South Wales and reported 'you're never going to believe it, but the bloke that interviewed me is exactly like the man in your painting'. Was this just a good ploy, or an indication that the job should be accepted?

What struck Calli most about 'The Game of Illusion' dream was the hand in the sky, the voice and the glowing quality around the man.

I live with voices, they tell me all sorts of things. This was a very strong voice, commanding. We moved to New South Wales in December 1990 and I have no regrets. It was the best thing I ever did in my life, because it was through moving that I finally put my childhood to rest.

After the move, a severe bout of neck ache led to a meeting with an osteopath, then a counsellor who was able to lead her through the grieving process for her mother: the final but necessary last step in her transformation. Calli completed the process through starting a painting of her symbolic rebirth.

The painting has been left half finished, perhaps because Calli no longer has the need to express anything further on the subject! Through her move interstate she has met with many like-minded people and has been able to catch up with

things she had always wanted to do. Calli now works as a clown at the Burns Clinic and the Cancer Clinic of a large hospital, entertaining children while they have their chemotherapy or their burns dressings changed.

I have a feeling I probably would have ended up with cancer myself if I hadn't gone back (to reconcile my past), because it was just eating me away. My health now is probably better than it's ever been.

So what was 'The Game of Illusion'? Was the dream scenery just a highly dramatic vehicle for the commanding voice and the directive to move south, to where the light is, or did it have a meaning of its own?

At the time I took the rivers to be emotions, but I didn't look any deeper. Perhaps I played games like 'I'm not moving', but I suppose we all play games.

The photo of Calli's painting had been out of sight for years until it was recently unpacked.

If I look at the painting now I can stand back and realise that life is a game, an illusion. Dice throws in any boardgame appear as chance happenings in life which take us up or down the snakes and ladders. Life is really a game, and if you can step back and see the whole board, you see life just takes us from the beginning to the end: and it's just a game.

### Jane's Interpretation

When Calli looked afresh at her dream painting it seemed to speak to her more clearly. Years had passed, Calli had settled various issues in her life and gained increased wisdom as a result. At times of crisis our emotions can cloud our perception, but from a distance, free from the emotional constraints of the time, we calmly see the big picture. Things fall into place. Calli understood enough of her dream at the time to follow its advice on a personal level, but it was only in hindsight that she saw the overall magnitude of the message she had been given.

Enormous insight can be gained by keeping a Dream Journal and reviewing it every six weeks or so. Simply reading through six weeks of dreams in one sitting will reveal a 'big picture' that may not have been obvious on a day-by-day level. With a degree of objectivity you can look back on the recent past in this way and see patterns in your dreams, your subconscious, your life. Flicking through your Dream Journal a year or so later, lingering over the vivid dreams, jotting down the odd insight, generating the 'big picture' of 'back then' is a powerful technique guaranteed to sharpen your perspective and show you how you have arrived at where you are today. You can capture your review in art: a painting, drawing or poem, perhaps. Collage works well in dream work and is an attractive technique for those who feel fumbly with paint or ink. Cut out and collect images that have appeared in your dreams, then arrange and glue them onto a poster in whatever way feels right to you. When you stand back to view your collage, the 'big picture' will emerge. As Calli's story tells us, creating a dream painting or collage has the power to heal and change your life.

Interpreting Calli's dream as an outsider, I would agree that the dream revealed 'the game of life'. Team game dreams often provide insight into the value of working as a team member, or taking on the role of leadership, working towards goals and so on. Competitive sport dreams may reveal our competitive nature, while dreams of endurance sport (marathon running, for example) may reflect our approach to 'sticking in there', to winning, to choosing the hard road or to achieving personal goals. Dreams of individual performance (dance, gymnastics, pole vault perhaps) may relate to public recognition, to individuality and much more. Life is very much an intense game as we become enveloped in the seriousness of competition, goal scoring, defensiveness, inter-relationship tackles or plans, puzzle solving and generally negotiating life's maze in our quest to find Centre. While 'game' dreams can give excellent practical advice about handling business, study or relationships on a day-to-day level, the 'big picture' of life on earth as a complex game diffuses our seriousness and frees us to make more appropriate choices.

So much for the 'big picture' interpretation of Calli's dream. On a day-to-day level I would focus on the fact that she perceived the rivers (emotions) as being the snakes (downs of life) and the roads (solid ground, direction) as being the ladders (the ups of life). In other words, she saw her emotions as dragging her backwards and her more conscious, rational self (grounded, directional, man-made) as taking her forward. The voice's advice to 'move near that man over there' reinforces the dream's suggestion that thought rather than feeling, at this stage in Calli's life, would take her forward. Why?

There are three reasons. Firstly, the man had a big head (a focus on the brain: thought); secondly, the commanding voice was male (Yang, symbolic of rational thought); and thirdly, his voice came from the sky (air also represents thought). I would have asked Calli what 'cross-legged' meant to her, but I would guess this to be a symbol of meditation and the dissociation process. (Meditation permits us to stand aside from ourselves, to be temporarily divorced or disassociated from the ego, and to see ourselves and our world more objectively.)

I would have advised Calli, on the basis of her dream, to consider whether her emotional reactions to her current situation were dragging her backwards, and to put more emphasis on clear thought, perhaps through dissociative meditation techniques. In moving interstate, she did finally put her past (and its dragging effect) behind her, so in many ways the dream advice was fulfilled.

# Ocean Dip

## Phillipa – The Old School 1994

> I can see my old school. It is going to be demolished and used for Aborigines. I feel I want to write a book, starting then (present time) and going back to my childhood (the beginning).

I had been, and still am, going through enormous changes in my life, including a change of residence to another town, our children leaving home and my husband planning to retire. In reality I had often thought of one day writing a book about my life to leave for my future grandchildren.

Phillipa brought her dream to our regular Dream Group, and in the ensuing discussion she came to the conclusion that the old school being demolished was symbolic of the old Phillipa being demolished.

I have broken away from the old way of thinking. Three days earlier I dreamt I was driving along looking for Enderley Drive. It was near the Italo Club. Through the Dream Group I realised that Enderley Drive was the 'end of the drive' and that I had broken away from a lot of the old Italian ways, symbolised by the Italo Club. It was the Aborigines that stood out in my life-changing dream because I couldn't understand why they should be there. Through our discussion I learned that they were symbolic of 'origins'. I knew that, as the dream suggested, I would have to write the book and go back to my origins.

It took Phillipa eight months to take action and start her book. Meanwhile other dreams highlighted the changes that were taking place within her. When she was ready she spent two solid months writing. When her book was finished she contemplated writing a follow up too.

Since I started writing the book I was surprised at what I discovered about myself and my family. It has given me a better understanding of my relatives, and I learned things I hadn't known. I can finally put it all behind me. All the past is contained in the book. I feel detached and separate from the person in the book.

I can now appreciate and be truly grateful for the good things that happened and at the same time the bad things no longer hurt and I can let them go. I am now on a path of constant learning.

### Jane's Interpretation

Since I was part of the Dream Group which helped Phillipa to interpret her dream, little further comment is required. What is particularly special about Phillipa's dream is that it can be seen in two short but significant parts. The first part is the symbolic dream image of the old school being demolished for Aborigines to use, while the second part is the accurate, on-the-spot interpretation of the dream. Phillipa essentially interpreted her own dream while still in it. You can't get more precise than that!

In writing her book, Phillipa took her life apart, brick by brick, demolishing the fabric of who she had become and exposing the foundations, her beginnings, her 'original' native self. She returned to her roots and, freed from years of conditioning, rebuilt herself according to her new perspective. Few are courageous enough to do this.

## River 11

## Moni – The Letter 1994

Mum and Dad came to visit us. We lived in a shop at the end of a long hallway. The hallway must have belonged to us too because it had a big, antique wooden entrance door at the front. My letter to them was sitting on my desk and I was very aware of its presence.

They were talking to us, but mostly to the children, as if nothing had happened, although they did seem to be going out of their way to be 'nice'. I realised I had two choices. I could slip the letter into the litter bin, since their attitude seemed to have changed, or I could give it to them. Leaving it sitting on the desk or quietly posting it later was not an option.

Dad was being particularly gentle at that moment, but I had no doubt as to what needed to be done. I handed the letter to him and said 'You have to read this'. He looked away muttering 'No, it's OK. I don't have to. I can't read well.' He then added 'Give it to Mum', as if in avoidance. I repeated, quite firmly 'No Dad. You have to read it.'

Maybe my upbringing wasn't so different from many others of my generation and English background. Some of the situations I encountered throughout childhood and beyond are the stuff of many a laugh-til-I-cry television sit com.

My father was the overly aggressive, overbearing, stick-in-the-mud type, whose favourite life avoidance pursuit was to sit glued to the telly while he ate or drank whatever was handed to him with rarely a comment. He had a rather paranoid streak which made it very uncomfortable to bring friends home from school. When I was about seven or eight I had the misfortune to befriend a girl whose parents were actively involved in the 'Ban the Bomb' nuclear protest marches. The criticism levelled at them and at my poor friend behind their backs made life less than sweet. In my teenage years I brought home a friend who happened to have a Polish surname and whose father was called Adolph. After weeks of Hitler jokes (yes, I did know that Hitler wasn't Polish!), it became easier to meet at her house.

My mother was an intelligent woman who chose instead to be a dumb martyr in her husband's presence and to bury whatever personal power she might ever have developed in the name of 'keeping the peace'. This was a ploy which we were all expected to embrace. Our purpose was to keep anything controversial, such as our opinions, from our father, thereby not only preventing his anger and 'keeping the peace', but also protecting our mother from ever having to face her fears in true relationship with her husband. We protected Mum and, in return, she pampered Dad. I don't remember a single hug or cuddle from Mum after the age of toddler-hood, beyond the goodnight peck.

Except, of course, I didn't always play the game, wanting to fight my own battles with my parents and to have the freedom to express myself as a separate person with my own thoughts and ideas. Although my siblings had their share of traumas, I most definitely qualified for the 'black sheep' label. I could tell the sheep from the goats though, and knew my true role: scapegoat.

All this is understandable. My parents lived in a rented room in a house when I was born some nine months after their marriage. Life was undeniably tough for them in every sense of the word. They hauled themselves through life and ended up doing very well in financial and material terms. I'm sure they tried very hard to relate to me, but they never grew beyond the stage of pointing the finger at me whenever their life was difficult. In their eyes, I had caused their financial and relationship problems by being born so early in their marriage. I was told this repeatedly, from a very early age, in the heat of many a moment as well as in the cold light of day. Fortunately, and to this day I don't understand how, I was exceptionally endowed with a belief in myself that was strong enough to say 'No, I know that isn't true', quietly to myself. With a weaker constitution I might have grown up believing them.

But understanding a situation is one thing, and still needing love and approval, especially as a child, is another. I excelled at school and at university which made them very proud of me, but criticism never lagged far behind. Our relationship staggered, through our occasional meetings, from one argumentative visit to another, and from one polite, avoid-it-all letter to the next. My poor father had very much hoped that I would go and do all the things he hadn't been able to do, as he had often told me. Yet, whenever I did achieve these things, envy reared its head. Expectations were dual: I was expected to be different, to achieve, to 'be a man', I guess, even though I was a woman, yet at the same time I was expected to pay for the trouble I had caused for the family through suffering, not through success. My mother put all my success down to good fortune, not to hard work: 'The trouble with Moni is, she's lucky and always lands on her feet'. She urged me that 'Manners maketh man, not brains'. My father was stuck between wanting to tell the neighbours how well his daughter had done and telling me that 'Little girls should be seen and not heard'. Success, in any of these ways, would always be undermined by my failure to achieve the opposite! I learned the meaning of 'tall poppy' this way!

Many years passed, measured by our docile, safe-news-only, air-mailed letters which criss-crossed the oceans as I went adventuring the world they'd never seen. I walked my fine line between fulfilling their dreams yet fuelling their resentment, carefully culling my reports home, editing my life because my reality would have been meaningless to them.

A few weeks before my dream, my parents came to visit me. I had been encouraging them for many years, but the trip out to Australia is, of course, one that requires some fortitude and commitment. My children were by now in their early teens, a handful of years younger than I was when I left home. I myself was older than my mother had been when I had departed the family nest. My parents adore children and, although I was not silly enough to believe that they would come all this way to see their daughter alone, I had hoped that their joy at seeing their grandchildren would open up the possibilities for a better relationship between us. Surely, I believed, after all these years and by virtually jumping a generation in time since I had last seen them, any hard feelings must have disappeared. In my own mind I had long since forgiven both of them for their previous words and actions, and harboured no ill feelings towards them. I had hoped that in the wisdom of their more mature years they might have come to a similar view. I was looking forward to their visit, but I was not entirely convinced that it would go as I wished. I prepared myself for the very best and for the very worse, so that, whatever happened, my world, as I had since built it, would not tumble around me.

So they arrived, and at first it went well, but time passed and they started to slip the odd recrimination about the past between the lines. Their resentment showed and it became obvious that, in their minds, I was still their child and should behave accordingly, with due respect to their expectations. Theirs was the privilege, being the parents, to pass judgement and question my actions back through the decades. Mine was, in their opinion, to listen and take note.

During the third week violence erupted. My father forcefully flung me against the wall and held me in a vice-like position because, apparently, he had disagreed with some mild statement I had made over dinner. Words flew in all directions and even my mother, until then relatively placid, struck out with clenched fists a number of times at my husband. Her punches were meant for me, but my husband stood in the way and I don't think she ever saw anyone but me. He took all the punches and later had the bruises to show for it. He asked her, while she was hitting out 'Why are you punching Moni like this?' and she replied 'Because she's my daughter. I can do whatever I like with her'. That said it all.

They packed their bags, told us they were leaving the next morning and shut themselves in their room. I was scared for our safety and wondered what physical damage my father might do to our car or our house. Thankfully our children were away from the house at the time. With my permission, my husband gave them two choices: they could sit and talk it out or we would book them into a hotel, send for a taxi, and they could leave immediately. After an attempt at a talk which became violent again, we ordered their taxi and they walked out of my physical life, probably for ever. As they stormed out the door I managed to get my mother's attention for long enough to say 'I know you find communication difficult, so I will write you a letter. You may read it, you may throw it in the bin, but I will also send a copy to my brother and sister. If you throw the letter away and ever find yourself wishing you had kept it, ask them for a copy. They will keep it for you. All you will have to do is ask.'

It's one thing to have dealt with a matter inside your mind, to have made the attempt to understand and to have forgiven everyone involved, including yourself, for the past. It's one thing to continue your life and to have learned from yesterday. It's quite another to find yourself confronted with people who have not let the past go, and who either wish to constantly retrace it, or whose behaviour and attitudes towards you, because of the past, need to be dealt with somehow. You can make peace in your mind, but what do you do when the person standing opposite you, or lashing out at you, does not have peace in mind? They are really crying out for answers and you are denying them, either by turning the other cheek or by stepping into your old shoes and playing the game according to their rules. Perhaps the only way to address the issue is to address the issue, but how do you do that when the person is screaming at you and hurting you? Words cannot be heard and subtlety is nowhere near the starting line.

I felt I had to write the letter. Nothing could be more painful than that last day when all hope of ever reconciling, or should I say building, a relationship with my parents disappeared along with their taxi. I had never had the kind of love and support that I had wanted from my parents, and now it seemed I never would. I hadn't realised, until that point, how much I had lived in that hope.

My husband and children, my true family, is entirely loving and giving in ways which I never knew were possible. For a few days all I could do was sit in a chair, completely stunned. I wrestled with myself. My philosophy had been to understand, to forgive and to let go: to move ever onward, having learned and thanked whoever was involved for what the conflict had taught me. Yet I also felt I needed to write the letter, to face their confrontation and answer their questions in plain language.

I finally decided the letter had to tell the past from my point of view, since this was something I had never done. They would never have listened without rage, and perhaps they wouldn't read the letter either, but I knew this was my task. I was selective. I picked out the good memories from my childhood, although they were difficult to find, and I balanced these with the bad memories. I tried to explain how I felt at different times and finally described how I felt about our relationship dynamics looking back with hindsight. I empathised with their situation and asked them to the stand in my shoes and empathise with mine. I gave answers to all their questions, replied to their accusations and told them that I only ever wanted their love.

Finally I said that both, or either of them, would be welcomed with open arms in the future but if, and only if, they came in peace.

It took me two days to write the letter and I felt better. I then wondered whether I should just throw it in the bin, as many a psychotherapist would recommend, and continue at ease with my own life, having expressed myself on paper. Something told me this would be pointless. I had effectively done all that before, bar the actual writing, and yet, confronted with my parents in person, the conflict remained as fiery as ever. I believed I should post the letter, owing it not only to myself, but, ultimately, to my parents as well.

Since the letter was couched in strong terms and I was mentally and physically exhausted, I decided I should at least sleep well and reconsider it when I was refreshed. The letter could sit to one side for a while.

I had the dream that night.

I could look at the dream symbolically, perhaps, and say that I needed to bring all the things in the letter to my own attention too. Wherever vestiges of my parents' attitudes remained buried in my own personality, they needed to be prised out and examined in the light of my letter: like looking at my own reflection in a glass whenever I look at my mother and father. The point was taken, but the dream begged for more.

In the dream, the situation was for real. I didn't know I was dreaming, so the question was crucial: should I hand the letter over even though they were acting as if nothing had happened and were being incredibly sweet, or was the content of the letter of such great importance that it needed to be delivered, no matter what? Faced with the situation and confronted with their sweetness in the dream, I knew Dad had to read the letter. I felt that gave us the only chance, albeit a slim one, of ever having a truthful and open relationship. They could stand there and be shiny all over on the surface, but our relationship would never penetrate deeper and touch the heart if we did not have the courage to look honestly at our past, shrug our shoulders in wisdom, release the burden, and start again with compassion. I'd had enough of superficiality. It was depth and honesty — or nothing.

On waking I knew that since I had made the decision in my dream to hand over the letter, believing the situation to be real and being totally satisfied with my action, that I should follow through and post the letter. I had no doubt at all about this. The dream did not add fuel to my fire; it added concrete below my feet. I felt steady, grounded, ready to take back what was mine: my full power to be who I am and to be entitled to say what has to be said. Above all, as in the dream, I knew that this was the only chance I would ever have to stake my claim for an honest and loving relationship, even though that claim might never be read, or taken up.

The moment I released my letter into the mailbox, later that morning, my shoulders lightened. It was as if I had been carrying another person all my life, and now I had only myself again. My energy soared and I couldn't stop smiling for days.

Three days after posting the letter I dreamed of my uncle, my mother's brother, who had died the previous month. He accompanied me on a walk, a much needed break. The road was quiet and something was explained to me at great length as he walked to my right, nudging his pushbike along as we talked. In answer to my question, he told me it was a five hour walk to his house. I was tired and sighed 'I don't think I can go that far, even though I want to'. Very kindly he explained that I couldn't go that far anyway, as this was territory beyond my entitlement just yet. Whereas I was tired, he was fresh and youthful. He took me to a room and sat beside me while I caught up on the sleep I needed. He seemed to be there to give me love and support, with a readiness to stay with me a while, until it was time for him to move on.

On waking I could recall none of our deeper conversation, but I felt refreshed, grounded and settled. I felt as if much had fallen into place.

I have not had one second's regret at my action, in or out of my dreams, and am eternally grateful for the courage which that dream gave me. My life has improved and opened up in many ways, especially in areas of asserting equal rights in all my relationships.

My husband has more empathy towards my upbringing, since I had underplayed the old family dynamics because they would have seemed unbelievable to others. His witness has been my gain, in belief that my perception of my past was not distorted, and that family life, as I knew it, was largely unloving.

I have not heard from my parents and don't expect to for a long time, perhaps never. They have written a couple of letters to my children: items of family news with no mention of my husband or myself. I feel I have extended the offer for a true relationship and can do no more. In my heart I love them, since I can see only the backgrounds they grew up in and the knots in which they have unwittingly tangled themselves; but loving them is one thing and deciding not to accept the hurt they offer in return is quite another.

## Jane's Interpretation

This is a good example of role playing in a dream, of putting ourselves on the spot, discovering how we really feel about something and then trying it out. The emotional response in the dream is usually a fairly accurate guide as to what needs to be done in waking life. The content of this dream clearly related to the problem that Moni took to bed, so the dream scenario is more literal than symbolic. Her options, in the face of her father's change of attitude, clearly run through her mind and she does not hesitate in carrying out the decision that is ultimately right and healing for her.

As always, other people in our dreams commonly highlight aspects of ourselves and naturally Moni's difficult relationship with her father over the years would have created aspects of her own character. In some cases she would have picked up his way of being and would now have to work at recognising these learned characteristics and deciding which to keep and which to let go. At the same time she would have built up a whole array of defensive behaviours or opposite attitudes to her father, the true origin of which could be properly assessed and valued by facing herself as well as her father. Moni's

dream symbolically shows the need to come face to face with the 'father in Moni', rather than to pass the buck.

The obviously symbolic part of the dream is the setting, since it did not relate to Moni's home. A shop, in a dream as in life, is a place of choice: we survey a range of options (goods for sale) and choose to buy or not to buy. The hallway in a dream can be suggestive of a rebirth (a long passage). The big antique door suggests that this issue of confronting or dealing with her father is an old one. Perhaps the door has been locked for a long time (antique, old), or perhaps the heavy old door is an allegory for the defence system Moni had built around herself.

While the dream's main purpose was to act as a vehicle for Moni's subconscious to role play and decide upon the action which was right for her, it beautifully illustrates the deeper symbolic aspects of a dream which have the potency to extend the life changes beyond addressing the relationship between two people and into the realm of healing and transforming the psyche of the dreamer.

## Ocean Dip

## Barney – Shot! 1994

I was approached by my friend Mike, who said that he needed help to blow up his boat. I was more than willing to help him, and we went in the boat to Green Island. I gave Mike the instructions for blowing up the boat and how to handle the police later on.

The plan was that once the boat was detonated, we would jump into the water and swim for the island. As we jumped out of the boat I was shot. I woke up, and feeling quite shaken, I looked for the blood, then realised that this was only a dream.

For a start I didn't believe in this dream business at all. Before this dream, I don't recall ever having one. I thought dreaming was a lot

of rubbish. However this dream shook me up, I can tell you, so I went to see my friend Heather just so I could share the experience.

I really feared that I was going to be hurt. What stood out for me in the dream was that Mike came to me for help, when normally he always went to Paul, a very close friend of his. I felt that his approaching me was a strange action.

Heather said that my dream seemed to say that I was 'green and impulsive' and that I 'isolated myself because of this type of behaviour' (Green Island). She knows me well. I couldn't see the point, to tell you the truth. I didn't make any effort to change until after I had a bad experience that seemed to fulfil the dream. That is, not until a week later when my impulsive actions got me into a fight that gave me concussion. Then I could understand the dream.

Personally I'm one of those people who calls a spade a spade and will use my fists when necessary. When I think people are having a go at me I'll drop them very quickly, or, I used to, before the dream. Mind you, I always give them fair warning: I'd speak once, then bang!

The fight, the concussion and seeing his first ever remembered dream fulfilled in the way that Heather had predicted was the turning point for Barney:

I started to change. I began to think before acting, and find that this pays off. I've decided that anyone can make an enemy, but not everyone can make friends. At times I have felt bored now that the excitement has gone, but found that people showed respect for my new laid-back attitude. This change was helped when I found people condemning the mongrel who hit me from behind, and admiring my self-control in not fighting back. Still, I wanted to get him, and was more or less waiting my chance, when I had three dreams that calmed me down. The effect of these dreams has caused a big change in my outlook.

Three sweet dreams! In one I was with my young brother in Heaven. He died with leukaemia, aged twelve when I was fifteen. I

never cried and refused to do that. Since the dream, when I knew that he was alive and happy, I have been at peace with myself.

Another dream was lovely too. I heard beautiful music and was aware that I was floating about one foot above the bed. I told myself to wake up and I did. I cried for the first time since my brother died and felt happy.

This happened very fast for Barney:

It was one week from the dream to the fight, then I had the three lovely dreams within the next two weeks.

## Jane's Interpretation

Everyone dreams, but not everyone recalls their nightly experiences. There are many reasons for this, but in Barney's case it's possible that he has been running away from himself for a long time. Fast, impulsive action without time for measured assessment of thought or the deeper levels of feeling, is a common self-avoidance way of life. In the end this can only be self-destructive, as shown in the dream.

In interpreting Barney's dream I would firstly ask him to describe Mike, because the dream concerns not only his relationship with Mike (self-destruction?) but also the Mike-like aspects of Barney. In what ways is Barney like Mike and in what ways does he play Mike's opposite? How could Barney benefit by killing off (shooting) the part of himself that plays Mike's games, that acts according to Mike's instructions? How often does Barney follow the Mike who lives in his own mind? Yes, the dream shows taking leads from Mike, or acting in Mike-like ways, is ultimately self-destructive. Before this dream, presumably, Barney saw Mike as friendly with Paul and unlikely to approach him. In the dream he realises there is a closer similarity or connection between himself and Mike than he thought. This is what brings him to his senses.

The beauty of Barney's first dream is that it causes him to slow down, to pause for thought, to begin to weigh up life's

conflicts rather than to act impulsively. As soon as he allows these moments of reflection into his life, he is ready to meet and heal his past. What is amazing in Barney's case is how quickly he allowed repressed grief from his brother's death to surface, opening himself to peace after so many years of avoiding the issue. What a life-changing gift!

# On Precognition

A precognitive dream is one in which we glimpse the future, either literally or symbolically, witnessing details which are later verified. Once the waking life event occurs, we may look back and say 'Yes, that was a precognitive dream' with varying degrees of certainty. The more literal precognitive dreams are easier to confirm, detail by detail, than the symbolic kind, although the dreamer always knows.

If the event occurs exactly as seen in the dream, it may be simply because we did see the future. Perhaps, on the other hand, we believed what we saw and made the future match it by virtue of our own actions or thoughts. We may see a 'good' scenario and gather enough confidence and inspiration from the dream vision to go out and make it happen, often without realising we have created our own future. Alternatively we may be horrified at the events we see in what we perceive as a precognitive dream, yet accept them as inevitable, thereby bringing them about through our own negativity. Often we have a good enough subconscious grasp of the likelihood of future events based on the present to project ahead and give ourselves fair warning, or hope in our dreams. Depending on whether or not we heed the warnings or flow with the hope, our dreams may or may not manifest as 'real'.

When our precognitive dreams are couched in the language of symbolism, or need an element of interpretation

to match waking reality, it is more difficult to 'scientifically' confirm precognition. In the end we have to remember the ground rule of dream interpretation: 'It's the dreamer's dream'. Deep down inside, every dreamer knows the meaning of his or her dream. Translated into our waking language (English, Japanese...the language of logic, technology and waking world perception) we lose much of the dream's significance, especially if we have forgotten how to move back into 'dream language mode' while we are awake. When a dream is interpreted, either by an interpreter or by the dreamer's waking self, the dreamer will recognise a 'correct' interpretation by a strong gut reaction. Touching the meaning of the dream brings a resonance which ignites a deep inner voice of confirmation. This is true for every dream, but when we live through an event which we have experienced in a symbolic precognitive dream, we just know the connection, because that same deep recognition is contacted.

As a precognitive dreamer myself I am aware that I experience varying degrees of precognition as described above, including literal and detailed preview, as well as witnessing events which are happening simultaneously to my dreaming (telepathic dreaming). These experiences are shared by many people and are far from unusual.

In this survey of life-changing dreams, we have an interesting juxtaposition: six dreams had strong aspects of precognition, or apparent precognition, yet they were also considered to be life-changing. While an event that is apparently 'fated' may be truly life-changing when it occurs, how can the original precognitive dream itself be perceived as the key to changing a life if the change was destined anyhow? These six dreamers have looked back and identified their life-changing dream as also being precognitive, yet they see the dream, not the event, as being the life-changing trigger.

# Ocean Dip

## Annie – Luke's Story 1993

My husband and I were sitting in the doctor's office being told we were expecting a baby in November. I could see myself sitting in a hospital bed waiting to go to theatre for a caesarean section. Then I could see a son being held up. He looked exactly as I thought he would. The dream ended with my husband and I crying and saying 'He's perfect'.

My husband and I had been married for seven years and had a wonderfully close and loving relationship, despite our terrible sadness at our inability to conceive a child. I had been diagnosed several years before with endometriosis and had a badly scarred pelvis from two major operations. We had conceived a child in 1989 by IVF in Perth, but I miscarried at ten weeks under very traumatic circumstances. We then moved to Tasmania and continued on the IVF program with many unsuccessful attempts at a pregnancy.

We applied for adoption sometime in 1991 and were accepted in November 1992. We were awaiting allocation of a boy from the Philippines and had all but given up hope of conceiving our own child. Our doctor advised us in 1992 that we were coming to the end of our time on the IVF program and he didn't think he could help us any further. I had given up hope that IVF would work for us.

My dream was a very vivid experience, almost like a vision. The dream had so much impact on me because through all our years of infertility I had never experienced a dream which was so clear and positive. In previous dreams involving birth I never reached the point of delivery: they always stopped short of this.

The moment where they held my son up really stood out in the dream as, in my heart of hearts, I always felt a son would come into our lives, be it an adopted son or otherwise. My interpretation was that I should clearly try again on the IVF program and that I would be safely delivered of a healthy son by caesarean section. Without a doubt I felt this dream was an omen of future events.

I had a hard job convincing my husband that we should embark 'yet again' on the IVF program as it would be our ninth attempt and he was worried I couldn't cope with more disappointment. Once he was convinced, I made an appointment to see the gynaecologist to convince him to put us through once again. This was January 1993 and we were leaving for a six month working holiday in April. I felt in my heart I must act fast and try again before we left for England. Eight weeks later we commenced the IVF program. I worked hard at getting myself fit and doing everything in my power to ensure we had the best possible chance of success.

Just as in my dream, I had a caesarean section and was delivered of a beautiful, healthy son, Luke, in November 1993. Every day I look at him and know he was meant to come to us at exactly the time he did.

## Jane's Interpretation

'Ah, a wish fulfilment dream,' some Freudians would say. What are wishes, anyway, but dreams which require action to make them real? So often wishes are written off as fantasy, as if we shouldn't have ideals, plans or hopes, let alone aspire to them. Which is it to be: accepting mediocrity because the general consensus is that 'it can't be done', or believing that you can have what you want and making it happen? How is Annie's dream for providing an inspirational answer?!

When I hear dream interpreters say 'wish fulfilment', I cringe. How shallow a thought! How totally disempowering! If a dream holds a perfect picture, or even a shadow of something you want, it is better to try it out, whether or not you fully succeed, than to write it off and never know how life might have been.

Symbolically I would notice the dream's emphasis on perfection and its sense of destiny, and suggest that whatever their relationship created, whether that was a child or a symbolic baby such as a joint business, an adopted family, a beautiful garden or a special understanding, all would be perfect and exactly as it was meant to be.

# River 12

## Jaquie – Working with the Inner Self 1978

> I was driving my car to a big city hospital many miles from where I was. I was going for an interview for a nursing position. As I parked the car I saw a sign bearing the name of the hospital concerned. I then found myself entering a small, older type brick building which was separate from the main building. I was shown into a waiting room and distinctly heard my name called. I then found myself in a room facing a long wooden table with three women sitting behind it looking very efficient. One I remember registered strongly as she came across a bit gruff. I somehow got through the interview and was told to report back on 4 February. I left the room feeling happy at how easy it had been.

It was in October 1978 and I was employed at that time by the social services to be a support network for the disabled who took holidays at this particular hotel in Avon, England. The hotel was up for sale and my job was no longer a viable position. I was having to leave in the beginning of the new year. I wanted change in my life very much at that time, but I was not sure in which direction to seek work, or in which area.

Just prior to going to Avon I had been through a messy divorce and was working full time in district nursing. My parents, who were aging, were pulling at me to go and live with them and look after them. I was in my late twenties.

At the time my whole being had felt that would be wrong and that I needed to move forward, so I had applied for the job in Avon and was initially turned down for it. I then had a dream which told me I would get the job, and indeed they rang me to say the chosen girl was not suitable and would I be prepared to take the job now? So I did.

I'd set myself in motion for change from that time forward, so that when the Avon job was folding I didn't want to go backwards. I felt I had set myself a goal and needed to keep going with it. I had a concern that I would find it easier just to slip back, to go back home and look after my parents, because I couldn't see a way forward at that given moment. I wouldn't call it fear, more concern that I would be taking a retrograde step rather than a more positive one. So the hospital dream came at the most important point, I think, for what was going on.

Jaquie's experience of precognitive dreaming gave her the incentive to follow through her hospital dream:

What stood out for me was how clear the dream was: the name of the hospital, the interviewing board and the date given. I had actually been toying with the idea of nannying or housekeeping, not nursing at all. Somehow there was a knowing that the message was a strong one rather than being a dream concerning a past situation, as I had been nursing many years before taking the social services post. Because of its clarity, I decided to test it out, and wrote to the hospital in question to enquire about nursing posts and courses. This was the morning after the dream.

There was no reply to my letter immediately, but then they wrote back and said they had courses available. At this point I felt confident that changes were awaiting me. And by golly I was right!

I applied for a course and went to the interview. I found the hospital with no problem at all. I seemed to know exactly where I was going although I really didn't know that part of the country at all. The interview was exactly as I had dreamt it. The lady with the glasses, from the dream, was the one who ushered me in. She was very gruff and stern, exactly like the lady in the dream. I seemed to pinpoint to the middle lady when I actually went to the interview. Somehow or other I had resonated with her in the dream so I chose her to resonate with on the interview panel! There were three ladies behind the board desk altogether and everything went well. I started at the hospital on 4 February, as in the dream, which was the first day of the operating theatre course I had been selected to do.

A week after I started at the hospital I met Graham in the pub that was directly opposite the hospital. From then on my life set off on a different chain completely. Following my divorce I had spent a couple of years really hating men and everything else that goes with marriage, but Graham just seemed to be right for me, yet he had everything that was wrong for him. We were very, very happy. He became my husband: I refer to him as my 'first' husband because my original marriage had been completely wrong.

Five weeks after we got married Graham was diagnosed with leukemia and we were told we would not be able to have children, but I had another vision dream and our son was born five weeks before Graham died. We had been married for three years.

Just meeting Graham was a whole new growth area for me. He taught me about being feminine again and I started to enjoy life and to get back my confidence. So he was very much a key figure in my life and really did change my life around.

Although I think meeting Graham was the main change resulting from the dream, I did learn a lot just by going through the theatre course. I learnt a whole new aspect of nursing which led to surgical nursing. This, in turn, helped me so much more when I was working with patients because I'd seen what they'd been through on the table and I could equate that with what they were going through and with the after care that they needed.

I've been psychic since I can remember and it used to be a bit of a game that I could see blue smoke coming from my hands when I used to touch the patients. I'd think 'Oh, this is good!', and my healing work just evolved from there. When I came out to Australia I was led to the Federation of Healers and into the spiritual healing I'm involved with now.

At first I worked in operating theatres here for three years, taking a year out to do counselling and to explore the healing and spiritual part of who I am. I wanted to learn about centring and balancing. The whole thing happened, I believe, to allow me to reflect back a little bit, to see how I had used the opportunities that had come to me. It was like a year in retreat, risky, but I've enjoyed it.

I am married again now, and I had many visions right up until the marriage. My present husband is not into it at all and somehow it didn't seem right to bring it in, so I lost a bit of it. It's beginning to come back a bit more now, and through reading *Sleep On It and Change Your Life*, and getting back into learning about my dreams, I'm starting to do it again.

I listen, and I follow. I applied for a job recently and when I got called for the appointment, I was everything they wanted. When I left the interview I was so sick in my body I really couldn't wait to get home. I thought 'my body is telling me something is not right'. That night I had a dream which was quite complex, but I interpreted it, and knew that I couldn't take the job. As soon as I turned down the job I got more and more home-based clients so I didn't need to take work anyway. The dream certainly helped me change direction.

Looking back over the years, because of the sequence of events that followed, I am delighted that I followed the hospital dream by taking the course of action that I did.

## Jane's Interpretation

If there is also symbolism in Jaquie's dream, it would be this: the dream ends with satisfaction and a feeling of a job well done, suggesting that the dream action is worth following. Symbolically this means staying in control (driving the car) and moving ahead (many miles from where I was). Jaquie was not to stay put or go backwards, as she had been contemplating, but to move forward.

While the dream advises her to go back to nursing, the double symbolism also refers to the healing (hospital) that would result. When she parked the car, Jaquie saw a sign bearing the name of a hospital, so the double meaning becomes 'just follow the signs'. The older building may have been symbolic of Jaquie's previous (older) work, nursing, but because it was situated separately from the main building it represented studying or working within a branch, or a different or smaller sideline of nursing, perhaps away from the mainstream. The number three tends to present in dreams as a 'whole', the body, mind and soul. The three women symbolically referred to development in all three areas for Jaquie, with a slight warning that one area (gruff) might need some careful handling.

With such a 'feel good' dream, Jaquie took the obvious and most positive course of action to discover that the dream was at least literally precognitive, if not symbolically so too.

# River 13

## Cassandra – Caught in the Fence 1986

> I dreamt that I saw the horse next door all tangled up in our border fence. It was so clear that I didn't even hesitate. When I went down to see my horses I just simply took the wire cutters and a halter. It was in a paddock that we can't see from the house so I had to walk a fair way. But there she was: the exact same scene that I'd seen in my dream presented itself to me then. She wasn't hurt, I just cut the wire out from around her legs and I took her home.

It's the precognitive dreams I've had which have changed my life and my way of thinking. I used to be pretty cynical. I'm a bit of a sceptic and I don't believe just anything I see, but when those sort of things happen it opens me up to not being so narrow minded and I can listen to people without being too cynical or judgemental. There might be other things that aren't really unnatural, it's just that we don't know much about them, that's all.

This was the first really precognitive dream that I can recall, although I might have had more of them when I was a kid. My precognitive dreams are different to my other dreams in that they're very clear and they make complete sense.

For example, a week or so ago I dreamt that I kept all my horse feed in the chook shed (which I don't), and I dreamt that my horse had got in and eaten it all. That's very dangerous for horses.

They usually die if they get into something like that, but he was alright. He ate all his food and had a wonderful time. I knew the dream was not precognitive because the feed was in the chook shed, which it never is. I wasn't worried that he was going to break into the chook shed at any time and get the feed because it's never kept there. Had I had the same dream but in the feed shed, I would have been very wary: watching everybody going in and out of the feed shed all the time, making sure they locked it.

I knew my 'Melbourne Cup' dream to be precognitive because it was really clear and sensible. The dream voice said 'Redor by five lengths'. On waking up, I said 'This is it!!!' and told my husband 'I think I've dreamt the winner of the Melbourne Cup!'

I didn't know anything about the horses in the Melbourne Cup, so we got the paper that morning and he looked through, but said 'No, there's nothing in here about Redor. Never mind, we'll just look through the whole day's program at Flemington'. There was nothing, not a race at all with Redor in it, but there was a horse called Redonicus in a steeplechase. Well, the first part was like Redor anyway!

At work I told a friend who was a real gambler that 'There's a steeplechase before the Melbourne Cup today and I dreamt about this horse and I think it's Redonicus. I'm going to put five bucks on it'. I never bet usually, but I thought I've got to tell someone, because if this comes off, I can't not have mentioned it! We went into the canteen at morning tea and listened to the race. I had put $5 each way on it.

I heard the same voice as in the dream say 'Redonicus by five lengths!' So, I had the name slightly wrong, but I had proof because I had told people. That's the only time I've ever won!

Cassandra works with horses and is used to communicating with animals while she is awake:

I don't know whether there is such a thing as telepathy with animals but I'm certainly aware of them all the time, because they're such a big part of my life. When you're dealing with horses as closely as I am all the time, you almost get to think like a horse.

Being herd animals, they are really sensitive to those around them. A horse can be a hundred metres away and another horse will be able to notice its intentions from the way the body is standing and the way the muscles are poised. They're ready for flight all the time because running is their only defence. They can detect the tiniest difference in muscle or body posture and be alert and ready to run. I'm often in the position where a horse is just about to step on my toe when I'm not even looking at it and I'll know to shift my feet.

Since Cassandra has opened herself to accepting a broader view of reality, she has been able to look back and remember other incidences from earlier in her life.

I was about fourteen or fifteen and had tried and tried to play the guitar, but I couldn't make any sense out of it or read music. Then one night I learnt in my sleep exactly where to put my fingers. It was only three or four chords but in the morning I woke up, immediately picked up my guitar, and it worked! Those four chords were so basic that I could play just about anything. I've been playing ever since because it relaxes me, and I never did take lessons. I just accepted it at the time. Maybe I had just read something about it subconsciously, but I told Mum how I learnt to play this guitar and she believed me.

Mum has had precognitive dreams and feelings. When my brother had an horrendous plane crash she was lying on the bed in the afternoon having a rest, but wide awake, when she heard him say 'There's a problem' and that's all. She knew there was something wrong. He was told he was going to be a paraplegic, but we all prayed for him and he's a pilot in America now. He's actually written a book about his experience and got it published.

When I was a kid it used to really put the wind up me if I dreamt of Grandma because she was dead. I still dream about her but it's not threatening any more. When people are as clear to me as in my precognitive dreams, then perhaps they may be there in spirit, but when they're a bit fuzzy I'm not so sure. My 'Horse Caught in a Fence' dream took place just before my son, Robby, was born and I guess it has affected how I've brought him up.

I try to encourage him to treat everything that's not quite so normal as normal. A very good friend of ours, Helen, an older lady, was dying of cancer. A couple of weeks ago my son said to me 'Mummy, I had a frightening dream last night about Helen'. 'Why was it frightening?' I asked. 'Because I saw her spirit go up to Heaven,' he answered. 'Well, that's not frightening. She is dying and she'll die soon,' I explained. Anyway we went over to my mother's and she said 'I've got some news'. I said 'Helen died. Robby told me this morning'. I turned to my son. 'See Robby, this lady was coming to say goodbye to you. There's no need to be frightened. I was so tired she couldn't get through to me!' I think it's important not to be scared about things like that otherwise he'll get a closed mind.

I don't want to inhibit Robby's subconscious and his dreaming, because you can really have problems when you do that. I'm encouraging him to talk to me about his dreams so we can sort them out, but also to learn to trust himself. In this way he'll grow to act on his dreams.

I'm more open to everything now, but the old cynical part of me steps in when people start setting themselves up as demi-gods and making a heap of money out of it. If I had that gift of being really psychic, there's no way in the world I would charge anything for it. I believe in the teachings of Jesus and Budda, and they didn't get money out of it. I've read a few books that have put me off reading anything about metaphysical matters. I just read the basic books and think my own thoughts as I go along. I'm open minded but I trust my intuition a lot more now, and that is something which has grown since my dream.

I'm a very practical person. I regard the odd precognitive dream as a handy way to get me out of a bit of strife and I'm inclined to believe in reincarnation because it makes sense that you come back to learn more. I try to act on my dreams now.

Overall, it's balance in the equation that seems to attract Cassandra now:

I think it's important to learn from your waking life as well as from your dreams. I believe that whoever's in charge up there will fit the

burden for your shoulders, but it is good to harness our subconscious experiences too. Wouldn't it be wonderful if we could be technologically advanced but still have all the spirituality of Aboriginal people?

### Jane's Interpretation

Interpreting this dream symbolically I would have seen the horse either as representing Cassandra's work (since she worked with horses) or in the more universal dream sense as symbolic of her passion. The border fence would be symbolic of the limits Cassandra perceived in her life, and the horse's legs would represent mobility and freedom. The dream meaning would become 'your passion for life is feeling restricted. Overcome this either by recognising your limits, or by extending them.' However, in Cassandra's case I feel this interpretation is probably irrelevant. This obviously telepathic dream fulfilled its dual purpose: the horse was rescued and Cassandra's mind was further opened.

## River 14

## Daniel – Warning From Daniel 1985

I was in a forest and a very strong wind came about. I looked up at the trees and I could see them moving strongly. As I stood in awe I had this feeling that the strong wind would cause one of these massive conifer-like giants to be blown down and cause terrible damage, but I was a witness. I had this real, innate knowledge. 'You know what's going to happen, Daniel, your job is to warn someone. For the moment, there's no time, just watch.' All this took place in about three seconds. I witnessed a tree come down and hit Andrew, the leader of our church, pinning him to the ground and crushing his right arm.

I was made a deacon in a large Christian church, although I didn't think I deserved it and I still don't. I was very spiritual then, much more than I am now, with my head more concerned with Heavenly matters.

When I became a Christian I started praying and things started happening in my life. I was like a spoilt child: my dreams were being answered. I was having a wonderful time and things like this dream had a special significance to me. I was like virgin ground so I was ready to receive these seeds. Nowadays my mind's filled with so much garbage that I don't think I'm a very good receptacle for such dreams.

I woke up remembering this dream like it actually happened to me and immediately wrote it down. I knew, I was very aware, that I had to go and warn the pastor. Everything hinged on me taking action. If I didn't, I didn't know what the repercussions might have been. I hear people talking about dreams warning people not to go on an aeroplane, and they act, and then the plane crashes. I had the same feeling of responsibility.

I had a childlike reasoning based on insight, that because I was God's servant, he enabled me to be used by him. I was just a messenger, nobody special.

So, how should I warn my pastor? I thought 'Hang on, just calm down. Don't make it so emotional. Why should I drive all the way over there and warn him? Maybe if I just go when church is on, then I can tell him and there'll still be plenty of time.'

So I went over to a session that I didn't normally attend, armed with all this fresh in my mind. I didn't need to read from the script because I could remember all the details after having written them down. I didn't know how I was going to get to talk to this guy because I'd never had any time speaking with him, even though I was a deacon. The church was huge. I prayed that if this was important for me to tell, then God would make it easy for me.

I was in an area of the church where the public go, but for some reason he was walking past and he saw me and he said 'How are you, Brother Knopke?' 'Good,' I said 'but I came over this morning because I've got something important to tell you.' He made time for me and took me aside. So I told him the dream, thinking this great spiritual guru will know what it's all about and say 'Ah, well thank you very much, that gels in with what I've been thinking,' but he said 'Well, what do you think it's saying?' It amazed me because I didn't have any doubt in knowing the interpretation, yet he needed me to interpret it for him.

Even when I explained the dream it still didn't seem to hit home with him. I told him that the tree pinning him down and crushing his right hand meant that something was about to happen and it was going to hit his right hand man. Now I thought maybe his right hand man was his son. I didn't really know who his right hand man was, but he knew.

I didn't hear any more until about six weeks later. Someone very important within the church told me that at a particular session he had said he wanted to thank Brother Knopke for the dream. All sessions were taped, and when I replayed it and heard him say how important it was in front of the entire church audience I realised it did mean something to him.

The church was subsequently rocked with the usual scandal the media digs up. For me the church started to crumble when I lost all faith in the senior deacon as a person. Later the pastor, Andrew, who must have been doing a very good job, was forced to move to another country. Obviously my dream had held a very significant warning.

Before the downfall, I used to have home meetings at my house, so people from the church could come in and pray and read the Bible. The senior deacon in question was the leader of all those home groups. Some church leaders were well-known for putting their palms onto the foreheads of those who go down to the front for prayer. I remember, on one occasion, watching this particular deacon actually push somebody over. I thought 'Take your eyes off this guy and just concentrate on God,' but kept thinking 'That doesn't look like God intervening here. This is not the Holy Spirit. This guy's pushing.' I became sceptical and this, combined with his poor personal behaviour, made it very sour for me. No longer did the things that they were doing in that church agree with me. I was not comfortable, so I left.

Warning Andrew about my dream was a really weird thing that I had to go out and do, but I knew, one hundred per cent, that it had to be done and I feel really happy that I followed my intuition. I'm aware that I'm watering the experience down, in telling you, so I'm not sensationalising it.

Although the church did at that stage crumble, it has been built up again. By getting rid of Andrew they felt they were getting rid of their problem.

My life has changed in that I left that church. Today, a Sunday, I went to a different church, so my faith is being stoked like the embers of a fire, just getting back again. I feel this church has got a lot of love, and that draws me rather than all the dramatic things that go on in a lot of other churches.

My dreams don't have a major part in my life any more and I really feel that's because I'm not spiritual enough. It just dried up after I left the church. I'd like to think that my dreaming might be some kind of gift that I have once I get into the spiritual side. When I return to that wavelength I'm sure I'll start having more relevant dreams.

Recently I gave a warning dream to my ex-wife, thinking it was for her. I get on fairly mildly with her, so I went to warn her and gave her the dream. I've since erased the full details from my mind but I did write it down for her. She thanked me because she knew the significance of my first dream about the church, but she added 'I really don't know how it can fit in and how it can apply to me'. It was a warning that someone was going to stab her in the back or do something pretty terrible to her. I was confident that she would know that I would be sincere: I wouldn't have wanted to look like an idiot by telling her these things if I didn't think it was important!

After about six months had passed she still couldn't recognise the relevance of the dream warning. As it happened, the dream was a warning to me over a maintenance action she took. I was 'stabbed in the back'. I don't think I was spiritually aware and in touch sufficiently to be able to understand what the dream was about.

Here's a thought from one of Daniel's flying dreams. Maybe it has the potential to change all our lives!

In this dream, about a year ago, I remember laying in the position of, say, Superman and then just levitating and moving at a medium to quick walking pace but doing all this with my mind. After the experience I recalled the tales of many Yogis and I remember thinking that it would be possible, and in time I'm sure that mankind will be able to move about just by willing it in our minds. My simple understanding is biblical: when God created the earth, so the Bible says, he spoke things into existence. We're supposed to be made in his image and I'm sure that if we can dream it, we can do it. If we can dream ourselves flying, then I'm sure we can achieve that.

Although not yet ready to fly, Daniel is using this principle to put a new and totally original family business into practise. He is, however, very aware of not using his dream gifts to his own advantage without due reference to his spirituality:

Dreaming would be useless to me as a gift unless I used that gift in some way that was connected to God. If I just took that information and used it for my own purposes and sold heaps of books or whatever and 'ripped God off' if you like, then I wouldn't really feel very satisfied. But if I did it because there was some kind of payback to God, my conscience would be much easier and I'd feel that I did the right thing.

Our dreams may be potentially life-changing, but I don't think enough people realise it. I read a book by a millionaire, Peter Daniels, who had studied what kind of principles successful people had in common. He concluded that our lives change from the books that we read and the people that we meet — and that's all. Now he needs to be contacted and told it's not only the books that you read and the people that you meet that are important, but your dreams can change your life too.

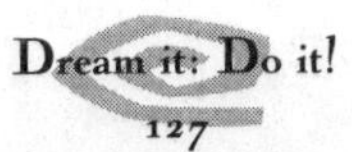

## Jane's Interpretation

If I had not known that this was a precognitive dream, I would have seen Andrew as symbolic of Daniel's religion, and the crushing of his right arm as a 'crushing blow' either to Daniel's self-expression within the church, or to his ability to give of himself within the church in the same way as before. The right side of the body in dreams often relates to our handling of the outer world, and our arms to our ability to express and give of ourselves. Was Daniel's faith in this particular religion under threat and was he beginning to feel crushed in his ability or willingness to serve? Was his job to warn Andrew or was it to heed the inner warning himself, the warning that his sense of religion and purpose was being crushed?

When trees stand in a dream forest they can represent a collection of people. These trees were huge, presumably quite old, so they may also have represented the church or its congregation. Strong winds make dream appearances when 'the winds of change' are upon us, when we are feeling emotionally stormy or when our sense of stability feels threatened. In this light, Daniel's sense of security regarding his religion may have been under threat from 'changes in the air'.

If this dream was entirely symbolic, and related to Daniel rather than to Andrew, I would have questioned Daniel about his strength of conviction within the church, asked which changes, if any, were in the air, and ask how he felt about these and his willingness to continue to serve this particular church.

There remains the observation that Daniel was a witness in the dream. Was he witnessing his own relationship to the church objectively, or was he aware of his role as a witness to future events within the church itself?

Daniel's conviction within the dream was that his role was to witness the future and warn Andrew. He carried this conviction into waking life action, and, since subsequent events proved the precognitive symbolism of the dream, the foregoing interpretation remains either a philosophical exercise or a parallel meaning to the dream. Precognitive dreams frequently carry a second layer of meaning: one personal and symbolically pertinent to the dreamer in tandem with the obviously precognitive one.

## River 15

## Harry – Three Tidal Waves 1993

> I was standing on a balcony and I felt a rumbling. I looked off the balcony and down towards the water. Along the beach front and to the left, there were three tidal waves coming through a bay entrance into a river mouth.
>
> I remember quite distinctly the building felt Mediterranean. The impact of the waves made no sound, there was just the feeling: oh, the feeling of it! I remember thinking how distinct the feeling was. The three waves went down through the river mouth and then disappeared.
>
> Then I turned around and went to the back door. When I opened it the waves had subsided and they were just lapping in little trickles, broken right down, at the back door. I had an overwhelming sense of 'It's OK'.

My dream came at a period when I was unsure, probably through a lack of self-security, direction and a lot of other aspects.

It was feeling the impact of the waves that really caused Harry to look deeper into his dream:

I've had many dreams that were significant but this one was so connected to the feeling part that it was eerie. It went through my body, like a feeling of knowing. It was as though I'd felt it before, but at the same time I didn't know what it was that was coming. It wasn't a past thing, it was a coming thing. It was an odd feeling.

I had discussed the dream with Jane Anderson and understood that basically I would go through three significant emotional periods or occurrences but that at the end I would be safe and secure.

Feeling that something was coming, but not knowing what, I waited for the significant things to happen. Those were my only steps: to wait for things to come at me. When they did arrive it was like ticking them off a checklist. As the events occurred, I recognised them. Other small things had happened, but there was no feeling attached, so I knew they were not the tidal waves. The real ones came with a hidden knowingness or feeling that was connected. It helped me to cope.

The waves came at roughly a year apart over a period of three years. Each affected the other which led on to decisions.

The first was my mother's death. The second was the effect of leaving my self-employment. Although it was a chosen direction, it was still a thing to overcome. The third tidal wave was the break up of my marriage.

On reflection I think it was all inevitable. The pattern was already there: it was set. It didn't govern my decisions and wasn't playing on my mind continuously, but after I'd made each decision, it then hit home and made sense. There was a knowingness about the whole thing. I'd get a feeling at the time of each event, but it's one thing feeling something at the time, and another thing sitting back and thinking about it afterwards, making the connections after the event.

A second dream, six months after the first one, was equally as important in changing my life.

> I was walking through a botanical garden on a guided tour. It was all nice and green, the trees and flowers and so on. We came across an old conservatory or glasshouse and the guide, who was a woman, opened the door. I was the first to walk in.
>
> The whole place was one big pool. The interior was old and dusty, but the water in the pool was crystal clear, although, by the same token, it looked very old. We were all taken aback by the whole thing. Again it was very much a feeling dream.
>
> We were all standing around and the guide explained about the pool and I remember saying 'Can we go for a swim in the

pool?', to which she replied 'Oh no! You're not allowed to swim in here!' Just as she said that a girl came rushing in and jumped into the pool. Everyone flipped out because of what the guide had said. We were all searching around trying to drag this girl out, which we eventually did. When we got her out she was embalmed in a cocoon. On cracking it open we saw it was like a reverse mould of her body inside, but coloured and textured like the underside of a butterfly's wings: all iridescent. I remember the feeling of seeing that. Bang: the colour! It was the only colour in the whole dream: like the inner coming out.

Most prominent was the woman jumping into the pool after the other woman had said 'You can't do that!', which was a real shock to me, and the breaking of the cocoon, seeing it turning into something beautiful — like a butterfly.

I discussed this dream with my wife and others and also rang the dream interpreter on JJJ. What struck me was that the female content of the dream was very strong. The female guide led us to the emotional pool, and also it was a woman, or girl, who jumped into the water. 'Diving into the emotional' was my interpretation, and it really hit home. I felt it meant that looking into my emotions and the feeling side is OK and safe. I shouldn't worry about what everybody else says, but just jump on in. 'The water's fine,' so to speak!

If anything, my health went down around the time of these dreams because of my process of thinking through the thing and bringing myself into turmoil. I tend to bring myself right down to bottom and then look at myself in the mirror and say 'What's going on in here?'

Whether these dreams have been total guidance, I'm not sure, but they have given me some sense of security throughout the whole trip. I'm happy now, though there are still a number of things I need to work on, but there's a good sense of security and freedom at present. What stands out is a sense of self-understanding and self-power, of doing it for myself.

People overlook the power of dreaming and take it for granted as something that we do. We're brought up thinking that we just

have dreams and not to take them seriously, but, if you're really feeling in a dream, which a lot of people don't do, that's the key. Touch onto the feeling side of it.

## Jane's Interpretation

Since I helped Harry with understanding his dream originally, my interpretation is woven into his story.

The first and most obvious comment to make here is that none of these people were experiencing any degree of crisis, major or otherwise, in their lives at the time of their precognitive dreams. Although Annie had been through much trauma and sadness over her failed IVF attempts, she had, by the time of her dream, reached a point of letting that go and was on the brink of adopting a baby from the Philippines. Jaquie was looking for a new job and was committed to moving forward in her life, but no great stress was apparent. Sue, Cassandra and Daniel reported no particular stress in their lives at the time of their dreams, while Harry was, in retrospect, feeling insecure about his future and his circumstances, but did not perceive himself as being overly concerned at the time.

How many of the events above occured because the dreamer made them happen, or chose to look back on their dreams as being precognitive? Which of these events would have transpired with or without recalling the preceding dreams? How much 'life-changing' was in the control of the dreamers, and how much was inevitable, simply previewed in the dream state?

In Jaquie's case, not only was the interview true to the dream, but she started at the hospital on the exact date given in the dream too. The important point to note, though, is that she didn't just sit back and wait for her dream to manifest itself. She had more direct plans: 'Because of its clarity, I decided to test it out, and wrote to the hospital in question to enquire about nursing posts and courses. This was the morning after the dream.'

It was the clarity that prompted Jaquie's action, and, as a previously experienced precognitive dreamer, her judgement was presumably good. To some extent, she made her dream come true, but other elements were apparently beyond her control, such as the date of starting at the hospital, the ease with which she found the place on going for her original interview and the true-to-dream faces and personalities of the interviewing panel. Did Jaquie bring these other factors into alignment through sheer power of thought, or were they always there for the taking? Was she shown a path? Was the choice always hers, or would it have come about anyway, in its own time? Did she accelerate her future by taking quick action on her dream?

In a similar vein, Annie's dream required definite action on her behalf before it could become true. Without the dream, she would never have taken the step of deciding to have one more go at the IVF procedure. The dream could not have become a reality without Annie's action. Yet she did become pregnant, the baby was a boy, he was born by caesarean section and he was born in November, all as the dream had shown. What caused such definite action?

Sue's action was equally as convinced, even though she was happily married at the time she received the dream: 'I was shown that my husband would meet another woman…I was then told that I was not to have any more children…I had a tubal ligation performed as soon as it could be arranged, which was only a few weeks later, even against the wishes of my then husband.' Sue's dream has been used in this book as an example of following instructions given in a dream, but time proved, in Sue's eyes, the wisdom of her action, when the other elements of the dream occurred true to detail, including matching her husband's new woman to the looks of the woman in her original dream. Sue felt the precognitive aspects of her dream served as a warning upon which she could base important life-changing decisions to make her future, within the limitations of the predictions of her dream, more manageable.

Absolute belief that their dreams were precognitive was a common factor among these dreamers, with the exception of Fiona. There was no case of 'maybe', 'perhaps' or 'only time will tell'. Their response, in each case, was to take quick action.

Daniel acted fast on his dream by warning his pastor, Andrew, of imminent danger perceived through his dream. One dream, apparently, served to change at least two lives. As time revealed, media attention scandalised Andrew's right hand man which led to a crumbling of the church, Andrew himself fleeing from the conflict. The whole situation changed Daniel's life and attitude towards that particular church, as his story explains. Precognition enabled not only Andrew but also Daniel to take stock of his situation and act appropriately.

Fiona's action was equally speedy.

## Ocean Dip

## Fiona – Love and Music 1980

> The details of the dream are vague: always were. However, when I awoke, I remembered that I had seen Simon lying sick in bed. He was wearing the cantorial robes he wore in the synagogue! I was very upset because he was sick. My first thought on waking was 'Good Heavens! I believe I'm in love with him!'

I was living with my elderly parents, a situation which didn't suit me at all. They were becoming increasingly dependent on me, emotionally more than physically, and I couldn't summon up the resolve to make a move. I had known Simon on and off for years, but had never given him a thought except as a casual acquaintance. He was unhappily married and had numerous girlfriends, but had never shown any inclination to leave his wife. The general opinion was that he wouldn't.

About a year before I had the dream, he told me that he had always been in love with me. I didn't take much notice until a couple of nights later, when he 'attacked' me. I was furious, bawled him out and barely spoke to him for a year. During that time, he was a perfect gentleman.

The fact that I was so upset in the dream because Simon was sick made the biggest impression on me and caused me to reassess my attitude towards him. I think I must always have been subconsciously attracted to Simon but had put up barriers: 'Don't get involved with a married man!', hence my reaction when he made a pass at me. Eventually, in my dream, my subconscious took over.

I could hardly wait for the following Friday evening, when I went to the synagogue where I was a chorister. I wondered how I would feel when I saw him. But when I arrived, the choirmaster said 'Simon won't be here tonight. He's sick!' The dream was confirmed.

From that time on, I treated Simon differently. My dead uncle came to me in another dream and told me Simon was the right man for me and I'd better not let him go. Having once sent him off with a flea in his ear, I realised I would have to take the initiative. I started to become friendly again. He got the message and events took their natural course. Now we are married.

Everything Simon and I did was in defiance of the laws of commonsense and I have never regretted it for a moment.

## Jane's Interpretation

Interpreting this dream cameo symbolically I would have started by asking Fiona what Simon represented to her. He had offered himself as a lover in the past, and been rejected, so he may have represented a lost opportunity in love, a potential marriage, or Fiona's 'inner male' (Yang: outer world) side. He was also wearing his cantorial robes, so he could also have been symbolic of Fiona's involvement in the choir or the church itself. So many possibilities, and which of these was sick or waning, in need of nurturing, in Fiona's life? Fiona would have to have decided this according to her gut reaction. To have had the waking thought 'I believe I'm in love with him!' was probably a carry-over feeling of unity and identification from the dream. Isn't it grand, though, to dispense with the complicated symbolism and know that the dream, whether or not an allegory, was actually the beginning of a fairy tale?!

Fiona's story illustrates another aspect of the life-changing qualities of precognitive dreams. Seeing part of a dream confirmed in waking life is a powerful motivator to making sure the rest comes true too! Zohara had a similar experience, in which she discovered the house and block of land she had seen in her dream, and followed through by buying it.

## River 16

## Zohara – A Glimpse of the Future 1988

> I was on a hill looking across a gully to a house. It was small and made of wood. My partner was walking towards me with our three children. They appeared a little older than they actually were at the time. Everyone appeared very happy and the whole scene was edged with a shiny white light.

We were living a 'normal' suburban lifestyle and my partner had a secure job.

About six weeks later, while we were on holiday visiting friends, they took us up to see some land near theirs that was for sale. We had no intention of moving there. We walked around and came to the top of a gully. I looked back at the house and realised it was exactly the same one that was in my dream. I had been seeing into the future literally. The dream had given me such a feeling of happiness, and actually seeing it in reality now had an impact. Everything was very spur of the moment. Without even saying anything to Bill, he said 'I want to come and live here'. I agreed.

We bought the land and moved on to it five months later.

On the evening of the day we first saw the house, we went to some people's place for a barbecue. I took the baby outside in the night time because she was crying, and I had this most incredible feeling of anger go through me. I'd never experienced it before. I don't even think I could describe it. I've never been a person given to that kind of anger, but I could have cheerfully ripped or smashed anything near me. It just swept over me. Since moving here that kind of thing has happened on a few occasions with things that have gone wrong. Looking back, it was a pre-warning of things to come. However, at the time the dream seemed like an omen that it was the right thing to do and that we would be happy here.

Although I have grown spiritually since moving, and I believe we were meant to be here, life has been very different to what we expected. If I had a crystal ball, and had seen what was ahead, I doubt I would have had the courage to come here.

We had been excited about moving and looking forward to it, but even on the day we moved I started crying as soon as we left. It was about two hours before I could stop and I wanted desperately not to come here. I didn't understand it at the time, but looking back, I'd say that maybe I'd dreamt about it but blocked the memory. Maybe I knew what was ahead of me on some subconscious level.

We were dumped down here with no electricity, no power and three children under the age of five with one still in nappies. We still had to build our house. We were here about three weeks when my husband said 'I'm going to get a job so you'll have to do all this because I won't be home'.

The house itself was 20 x 20 foot and we lived in that for about twelve months. We finally got another twenty feet up but we still only lived, the six of us, in a 20 x 40 foot dwelling. Since Bill did go and get his job, I did a lot of the work myself. We hired a carpenter for ten dollars an hour and I helped dig all the trenches, the septic tanks, and so on. Perhaps it was symbolic, because it did turn out to be a complete change of life for me: complete renewal on every single level.

After moving we had several car accidents and my partner had a nervous breakdown. He's a labourer now, no longer allowed to do the managing side because of his breakdown. He's also developed rheumatoid arthritis, which is really bad. In many ways I was pulled along in the wake of Bill's situation, because what he was going through led me to anger and resentment.

Zohara mentioned that when she has a dream that is shiny around the edges, she knows she is meant to take notice of it. So why did the dream lead her into such apparent trauma?

I guess, looking back, a lot of things here just happened so that I could experience the dark side of myself. Up until that point I'd probably been a goody-two-shoes, which it was easy to be since I've always had guidance. I've always had a guardian angel sitting on my shoulders! My dark side has shown me emotions such as anger, even resentment and other feelings that were alien to my nature until we moved here. I can see that you can't help people in difficult situations unless you've experienced them too. It doesn't matter what it is you're helping people with, words are empty unless you've been through that experience.

If I'd wanted an easy life, I shouldn't have moved, but I couldn't have grown to where I am now if I had stayed where I was. I've kept contact with one old friend who came down to see us, and, although it sounds a terrible way to put it, she seemed very churchy. I realised how very limited her belief systems were. Maybe I would have been happy to have stayed in those same limitations, but all my life, each time I have got comfortable with a belief system, something has happened to push me out of it, or make me move in some way. I've never been allowed to stay static. I've only realised that in the last few years.

Now it doesn't matter what happens to me as I know its only for my own growth and my own benefit so I go with it. If you asked me what has happened in the last couple of years I'd say nothing, because I don't see anything as a problem. I just see opportunities for growth. This attitude makes life a lot easier.

My whole point of view has changed. I don't believe we have to go through all this struggle and karma any more. I think things have changed to the point where we can live and come from a state of being in grace, and we can learn through joy and insight. If we can choose to learn through insight we don't need to go through struggle.

Zohara's dream and the action she took led to her transformation through difficult times, but she also attributes these deep changes to the challenging nature of the geographical location of her dream house.

We live under a mountain which is definitely a transformational place. Most people who come here last three to five years then move on. We've been here for seven years. When we first came I went to the swimming pool one day and someone asked 'Are you married?' 'Yes,' I said, and they just laughed and replied 'Well you won't be in six months!' When people move down here they're lucky if one out of twenty marriages last. It's a place people come, they grow, then they split up and go in other directions. Even older people in their fifties go through divorce here! If they can understand and learn from their growth though, it's fine.

I have a sense of very deep peace and contentment here. No matter what's going on outwardly I can just stop, and within two seconds I know peace and contentment again. I also know that I'm not alone.

## Jane's Interpretation

A symbolic interpretation might suggest that Zohara was taking a distant view from above (on a hill) of her life: in other words, she was taking an objective perspective. Contentment, either as a family or on a personal level for Zohara, the dream suggests, could be reached by making life simpler (smaller house) and more natural (wood). The children may have been seen as older to give Zohara a feeling of future happiness. Zohara, however, knew that the shiny white light edging to her dream was a personal sign to look

beyond the symbolic. Being faced with seeing the actual dream house later confirmed her feeling.

In contrast to the fast action initiated by many of the dreamers whose stories appear above, Harry pondered the meaning of his dream. His final action was not a physical one, but a mental and emotional conditioning in preparation for the events symbolically predicted by his dream. As his report indicates, this was not a matter of making future events fit in with the dream because there was a feeling, or knowingness, that connected him to the events as they occurred. Linking future events to any precognitive nature of the dream, although not concretely verifiable in scientific terms, was irrefutable to Harry. He was able to withstand the emotional battering which might, without the dream, have exhausted him. In being able to look ahead he was able to change his attitude towards emotional circumstances on his horizon, in ways which ultimately changed his life too. In this way, precognition can allow us to plan ahead and make positive life changes from potentially devastating future events. Fore knowledge, even of exciting opportunities, can affect how we ultimately handle a situation.

In my own dream world I was offered a job, one day a week, with a company of which I had no conscious awareness. Specific details included the day (a weekend day), the hour and nature of the work and the name of the company. Ten days later, in my waking life, I received a phone call from a company with a similar (not exactly the same) name, offering me the same job, for the same day and hours. Without my dream I would probably have jumped at the opportunity, but I recalled that, in my dream, I made the point that I didn't want to work weekends and that time with my family was more important. I also felt the company was new, untried, and that I would be better to stay where I was. I contemplated the difference between my dream decision and my waking inclinations, discussed it with my family and a few close friends, and turned it down. I'd had the choice, because of a precognitive dream, to consider the job offer from a subconscious viewpoint and then to weigh this alongside my conscious reaction when the opportunity actually presented itself. In retrospect, although I don't know what the alternative outcome would have been, I feel I made the right decision.

We often stand on the brink of life-changing decisions, moments of action or inaction: go, stay, be bold, reconsider. We rarely know whether the small step we take will lead to big, irreversible changes, or whether the huge leap we believe we are making will result in only the tiniest splash as life blinks an eye and continues undeterred upon its original path. Precognitive dreaming, rather than being seen as a glimpse of inevitability, should perhaps be viewed as providing insight upon which we might wisely calculate, plan and truly create our future. Life change, like the future, is a matter of choice.

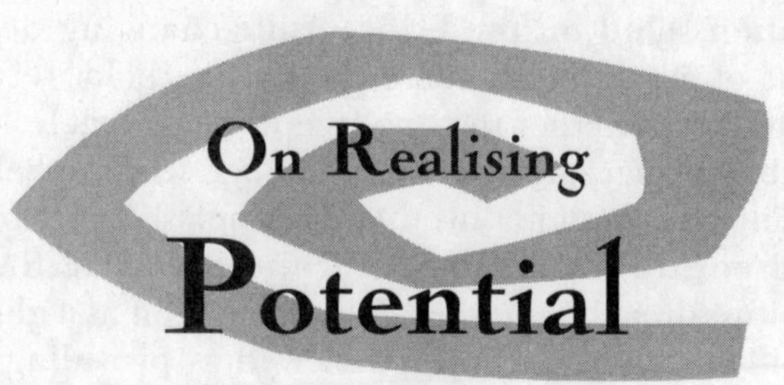

# On Realising Potential

*I feel my creativity has awakened and that I am full, like a rose in bloom.*
MICHAELA

*To my amazement, Brad is sorting out some paints. He suggests I look in the cupboard where I discover a brand of paints I'm not familiar with. They seem luminescent, which prompts me to say 'I fear my talent isn't quite up to the quality of these paints! I'd probably just waste them at present. Maybe in six to twelve months…' 'Stop putting yourself down!' he admonishes me. 'Just try them. You might surprise yourself! Fear of not being good enough stops the flow of your imagination. Just do it!'*
LEE

Many of the dreams in this book changed lives because they gave the dreamer a glimpse of their full potential, or showed them how and why they were restricting their development, or gave them much needed inspiration or motivation to 'just do it'.

Going for gold often requires the courage to break the rules, to act according to your intuition rather than society's expectations. Fiona's dream gave her the inspiration to go out and change her life, regardless of convention. As she remarks:

'Everything Simon and I did was in defiance of the laws of commonsense and I have never regretted it for a moment.'

Susannah was physically ill and emotionally run down. Life seemed to be dealing her the kind of blows that sap the self-motivation required to turn circumstances around. A deceased relative came to the rescue through Susannah's dreams, urging her to put her money into doing up her house as an investment to solve their financial problems. She also spent many dream hours teaching her an appreciation for the art of pottery — blue bowls in particular. This much needed dream inspiration fuelled Susannah's drive to further fulfil her potential.

Peter's dream provided the final motivation he needed to fulfil a dream he had held for two decades.

## River 17

## Peter – The Water is Perfectly Safe 1994

I was transformed into a situation which I remember as being a bus terminal which was familiar to me: it was in New Zealand. I remember coming across a fountain which was more like a waterfall, coming down from the side of a building. I was standing across the road, looking at it. There was a platform about half way up this fountain and the water was really turbulent underneath it. There were some little boys, lined up, along the platform, and there was an older man who was trying to coerce and encourage them to jump into this water. The water appeared to be hot. It may not have been hot, it just had that appearance. In other words, it was a dangerous situation to go into.

The man was saying to them 'Jump. It'll be OK,' but he was using really mean, foul techniques to do it. All I remember is going up to this guy and saying 'Hey, listen, don't do that, that's wrong. You shouldn't get them to do that, they're really scared.' He was really aggro about that, saying 'Hey, it's none of your business, you stay away.'

I went away and I kept on feeling guilty about the fact that these boys were being used by this older guy. He wasn't recognisable as anyone I know, neither were the boys. Eventually I managed to get up on the platform and I said to the guy 'You stay out of my way. Get out of my way. I'm not interested in you.' I went up to the first boy and I remember talking to him and saying 'Listen, it'll be OK. Everything's all right. The water is perfectly safe. There's no problem with the water. I will jump in it with you, and I'll lead you down the platform, down the ladder (there was a ladder that led down to it, like a diving platform), and into that water. Then we'll wash ourselves and then we'll be on our way.'

The significance of the bus terminal was in there as well: it appeared to be transportation out of that area. So gradually, one by one, I led these boys down into the water. We got into the water, swam and I said 'Look, see! It's OK. It's not going to hurt you. It's just that this guy was doing it wrong. He was trying to use trickery and deceit and lying.'

After that I can't remember much, except that there were some little girls that were in the dream before the little boys. I think the girls were being caned or hurt by an older woman. I can't remember the detail but I do know that I managed to stop this lady from caning and hurting them. Again there was no recognition of the older lady or the little girls.

I do remember quite vividly, in both situations, with the little girls and the little boys, everything was 'OK, come with me and I'll take you by the hand. You don't need to be whipped or hurt.'

I'm thirty-six years old. I was an adoptee at birth and I've always known that I was adopted. My adoptive mother died two and a half years ago and that really threw me out because I realised I would have to do something about finding my natural parents. If my adoptive parents were dying, it could be that my natural parents were dying too.

The only thing was that I didn't want to hurt my father. I remember as a little kid, my father would just encourage us so much and he would always try and do things for us and, like most adoptees, you feel very guilty if you think about finding your natural parents. You don't want to hurt your adoptive parents. Even my sister — I didn't want to hurt her.

I was wondering also whether there were brothers or sisters, and with marriage difficulties I really wondered about my past.

I was really feeling all that when I had the dream. I felt a real lack of identity. Searching wasn't foremost in my mind although it was something that I was contemplating doing.

I was burnt out after the events of the last two years. We've had a difficult business here, paying back debts. I was on sleeping tablets and I had just come off them about two weeks before the dream. At the end of November, just before the dream, I went to see the doctor and he said I was in a state of exhaustion. I had a constant headache, stomach aches, cramps, the whole lot. He just said to me 'You've got to knock off, you can't keep on going the way you're doing'.

What really struck me about the dream was the kids. I really like children. Unlike a lot of males it was always my dream to have children and to see kids badly treated, to see someone purposely trying to use children and abuse them, really affected me a great deal. It was a natural reaction of mine to go up and try and assist the children. I woke up thinking 'How can anyone do that?'

Peter had phoned me on the Dream Talkback segment one week after his dream, to ask my opinion and advice.

I remembered you saying, in the past, that the female figure is the creative figure, whereas the male figure is the logical figure. I thought 'Well maybe I'm still too logical. I need to became more creative'. In actual fact it wasn't totally that.

Your interpretation was that I was to have confidence in what I was doing. It was about having confidence and the need to identify little Peter. After talking to you it was just like 'OK. Do it. Don't muck around as you have done for about the last twenty years'. I've wanted to do this for about twenty years and I've always found an excuse not to do it.

So, with confidence, I sent away for my birth certificate. It happened so quick. It took only eight days to come back. The name on the birth certificate was so unusual that when I rang the New Zealand Directory Service I had my father on the line in a few minutes. It took a total of nine days between the day I sent the birth certificate away and the day I was talking to my father on the telephone.

I was going to New Zealand anyway so I made sure that I made contact with them while I was over there, although I was only there for one week. I'd met my father for a few days, then he said 'Come, round before you fly out. I've got a few people for you to meet.' In two hours I met my grandfather and grandmother on my father's side, two nephews, my full brother and my full sister. That was the day that I left for Australia. It was weird. And as of a week ago (January 1995), I've got a niece too! I'm sure if I wasn't so tied up with work (I guess I'm a bit of a workaholic) I'd be going through a period of shock now.

My mother had died two years ago, just after my adoptive mother. My parents had been married when they adopted me out and their marriage broke up five years later. My father remarried and had another son who was also adopted out. He's since found him. I saw a photo of him: his name is Peter, too.

Adoption is one of those things that you can never describe. Unless you've actually been adopted you can never understand it. That's not putting anyone down or saying that they don't try and understand, but it's very difficult to do that. I do a bit of writing, creative writing and poetry, so I put it into poems. I don't know whether it's a regret, but I have a feeling I just wish I'd done it earlier.

It's very hard to describe the feeling you have when you find out that your mother has died. I wrote a eulogy to her, a poem, which is called 'Gwen'. I wrote part of the poem for other people as well as for myself, just to let them know, because people do ask you how you feel and you've got to have some kind of answer for that. You can't just keep it to yourself because that's only going to do you harm as well.

GWEN

*Far flung stories of likeness past*
*So much away from my present caste*
*All messed up in an orderly file*
*All heaped on the puzzlement pile.*

*I've felt the pain of a mirrored mind*
*And denied a push of the likeness child*
*Now I've heard that the search is through*
*Now my thoughts will envision you.*

*To the mum that I never knew*
*Thank you Gwen for my life anew*
*Turn to my loss and a life to see*
*Close by your side, no escape, but free...*

I think I did mention to my father that the dream spurred me on, but he is very unemotional. I guess I'm unemotional too. I'm a mere male! I was quite embarrassed when I showed him the poem but he really appreciated it. I guess I'm really the sort of person who likes to keep myself to myself, except when something extremely personal happens: that's really weird, I know, but that's the sort of person I am. My father's a bit of a business guy so we keep in contact over the fax.

After the dream, and after I discovered my father again, I just went into shock and ended up again at the doctors. It was an extremely stressful time. I took it easy on the week's break and went sailing, fishing and all the natural things that I enjoy doing and so this year I'm feeling very strong. I'm riding my pushie every morning at 5 am for an hour and I physically feel a lot better.

I had another couple of important dreams before this one, one of which was about a new direction in life which you also interpreted for me. You said I've got to let go of my logical self and start being creative and have a change of direction and that started me thinking that I'd been working hard all year and thinking 'business, business, business' all the time. Where's my creative self gone and where has my personal life gone? The year before I had been thinking about the adoption and other issues and it spurred me on. I play in a band now. I had dropped out of music for a long time before that and I thought I'd better start playing music again, so I did! It's going very well. We have a residency at a local restaurant now.

Searching for my natural parents was a very stressful time but it was something that I had to do. It was also such a great way of improving my self-esteem. Towards the end of last year my self-esteem had just plummeted and I'm not naturally a person who's self-esteem is low. Adoption does affect people, but now I have self-esteem that I never even knew that I had. You just know who you are and you've got something to identify with so naturally your health is going to be better too.

## Jane's Interpretation

Peter's main feeling in the dream was distress at seeing the children badly treated, abused and driven to jump into the scary, turbulent waters. His reaction was to dismiss the old man and gently coax the boys into the water himself, in a loving, step by step manner. He also joined them on their journey, cleansing himself in the water at the same time. The need to go through the water was unquestionable, but the dream indicated the best way to approach the situation.

The old man was the 'hard task master' part of Peter. He was the driving force, the workaholic. Working hard was perhaps a way of denying his real needs, just as the 'hard task master' was perceived as using 'trickery, deceit and lying'. There is a time and a place for disciplining ourselves, but the dream showed the tender, vulnerable, childlike side of Peter (the little boys: his 'inner child') who was suffering from this approach. His 'inner child' was multiplied into a number of children in the dream simply to grab Peter's attention. (Dreams often emphasise a key symbol either by making it larger or by duplicating it.) Peter's business and personal life were under a lot of stress, and his 'inner child' was crying loudly for attention. This was a time in Peter's life to go backwards in order to go forwards. He needed to go back to his origins, enter through that turbulent water (turbulent emotions), cleanse himself and then be free to continue his journey. Peter needed to command his 'hard task master' to stand aside because his harsh demands were frightening the little Peter inside.

Little Peter had fears to face: the fear of what he might discover about his natural parents (given his own marriage difficulties), the fear of hurting his adoptive parents through revealing his need to trace his natural ancestry and so on. The grown up Peter needed to stop driving himself hard, take control and compassionately take little Peter's hand, identify with him (acknowledge his vulnerable, childlike side) and gently and confidently enter the water.

The confidence Peter felt in enacting this in his dream made it easier for him to do the same in his waking life.

'Then we'll wash ourselves and we'll be on our way,' he promised the boys. This indicated that the journey of the inner child, into the water, through the fear and towards discovering his natural family would free him to 'be on his way', to continue his journey forward in life. The setting was New Zealand so it was easy for Peter to connect the necessary journey with the search for his natural parents in New Zealand. The bus terminal underlined not only that this was a journey, but that it would represent a 'turning point' (as the buses turn around) in his life. Perhaps the word 'terminal' also reflected the 'end' of one journey: every ending signals a new beginning, as indeed Peter found by gaining the confidence to follow the dream.

# Ocean Dip

## Vi – The Tree 1990

> I was in a tree like a bird in a nest. I knew it was the tree of knowledge, of life. I was perfectly safe, completely enclosed and no-one could see me. I was receiving strength from the tree, making me strong. There was a beautiful light coming between the branches. I could hear the birds singing all around me.

My life was quite humdrum before the dream. I'd had a series of dreams, but none of the others were as vivid as this. It left me wanting to be able to understand more about the tree of life and all it could give me.

The interpretation was clear: it was time to stop sitting around. I realised I had to be in charge of my life, to gain knowledge in any way I could, through books and people. I had to get off my rear and start doing something.

I started the changes the next day and four years later I am still making progress. I feel my health and life have improved because the dream has made me more in charge of my life.

### Jane's Interpretation

Life is much simpler when our dreams give us both the symbol and its meaning in the same breath. The tree frequently appears in a dream as a symbol of the dreamer, its roots representing the dreamer's origins or earthiness, the branches being the dreamer's divergent interests, the growing tips his or her present development and so on. The tree analogy extends to the type of tree reflecting the dreamer's personality, its health the dreamer's state of health, its season his or her stage of life and so on. In other dreams the tree can appear as the 'family tree', or may appear to describe a clichéd feeling in the dreamer's life, such as feeling 'uprooted', 'out on a limb', full of 'dead wood', 'out of her tree' and so on. Vi did not need to consider these because she knew she was perched in the 'tree of knowledge'.

The birds, being symbolic of the soul, were singing, just as the dream suggests her very soul would become inspired through advancing her knowledge of life and involvement in it. Vi's dream felt safe and was sensually charged, vivid. This combination of positive emotion and heightened sensual awareness can sustain the dreamer for days, even weeks. I have often used a dream image to inspire me to complete a task or to give me the courage to make a change or take a new step, just as this dream inspired Vi to step out and explore her world.

## River 18

## Lee – The Mysterious Gift 1992

I'm contemplating the branches of a silver ash, through a window overlooking the street below. It's a dull grey autumn-into-winter day. Seated at a round oak table, Miss Venables regards me curiously.

'For next time paint me some pictures,' she says, 'so I can puzzle out where you're going.'

In my mind's eye, I see two small paintings. One is of a brilliant yellow and orange sunset. A silhouetted figure with a bundle and a dog is setting out along a roadway between tall poplars. Though ethereal, it's evocative of Van Gogh. The second reflects rays of white light from a crescent moon against a violet-blue sky turning indigo. I think of Vincent's 'Starry Night'. In the forefront, on either side, great plane trees with sturdy trunks, spread forth shimmering multi-coloured leaves to shelter the path.

As I'm imagining transferring these visions to paper for my next visit to Miss Venables, I become the figure leaning against the wooden fence-rail, staring at the moon, my dog Wolf-Moon by my side. It seems somehow appropriate that I'm wearing a black dress and veil. My tabby cat rubs against my legs, miaowing, beseeching me to follow her, which I do. The path stops abruptly at the cemetery. Someone steps out from behind a tombstone, startling me. Fear dissipates when I recognise Brad, dressed in his Edwardian wedding suit and white shirt with lace jabot. As if in benedictory gesture, he cups his hands over mine, then releases something. I'm bewildered as there doesn't seem to be anything there.

'That's right,' he murmurs. 'It's everything and nothing!'

Smiling enigmatically, he bids me farewell and vanishes into the depths of the cemetery.

I understand he expects me to choose my dream, finding joy in the process rather than the results.

Time passes…

I have joined an art class at a church hall. One day I get there early to find a man with unruly hair, already working at his easel. He looks like a well-known painter whose identity eludes me.

'It's the best time! Before the others get here,' he asserts heartily. 'This way, you can initiate your own project.'

He splashes paint about his canvass with such gusto, I feel intimidated so I seclude myself on the other side of the room.

Eventually, I gravitate towards him as his lively observations whet my curiosity. 'I find painting in the presence of others rather daunting,' I venture. 'You actually seem to enjoy it!'

'Of course! It adds a dimension of spontaneity and decision because it forces something else to emerge.'

I watch him dabbing pale pinky-gold and vermilion splotches across long green stems, creating a field of bright living poppies swaying in the wind. Again, I think of Van Gogh. Such self-assurance! If only I could absorb some of it.

Afterwards, he leads me into an old shed with a long passage way. It's rather dark and haunted-looking, though light streams in at the other end. Forgetting my companion, I wander through the first doorway into a store-room containing art materials. To my amazement, Brad is sorting out some paints. He suggests I look in the cupboard where I discover a brand of paints I'm not familiar with. They seem luminescent, which prompts me to say:

'I fear my talent isn't quite up to the quality of these paints! I'd probably just waste them at present. Maybe in six to twelve months…'

'Stop putting yourself down!', he admonishes. 'Just try them. You might surprise yourself! Fear of not being good enough stops the flow of your imagination. Just do it! Think about what I've said. You'll realise I'm right!'

He walks out the door.

I follow the light to a charming garden full of red poppies and a pond with water-lilies.

Opposite is a reception room crowded with advertising people. I slip amongst colleagues talking shop but can contribute nothing. Some are sipping a strange, turbid concoction. When another round arrives, I'm by-passed.

I decide to return to the garden. It really is time to accept the message and move on.

Who says it's the end of a relationship when someone dies? My husband Brad, a creative director, died several years ago, but he visits me in dreams to help me unfold artistically.

I was working as a freelance fashion artist, sometimes doing illustrations for advertising agencies, but mostly working for one designer who was very demanding. A few years before, I had cut my right index finger very badly, severing nerves. The damage was irreparable, making it more difficult for me to cope with fine, detailed artwork and to meet deadlines which are always a problem in advertising and the fashion industry. I was also developing more spiritual interests which led to more dissatisfaction with commercially orientated work which didn't allow me to express my creativity as I desired.

A few months prior to the dream I'd been in hospital for a short while with a couple of cancer scares and, prior to that, an operation to try to restore full use of my index finger.

There had been plenty of stress in Lee's life, leading up to 'The Mysterious Gift'.

The death of my first husband was a big shock. He had a serious disease, but he used to say 'I'll still be playing my pop records at 80', so I used to comfort myself by thinking he'd be around for a long time. There were so many things left unsaid. I sort of felt guilty afterwards that I hadn't seen it coming. (He died suddenly of a heart attack.) But we still carry on in dreams where we left off, so it doesn't seem so bad.

Added to all of this, all Lee's savings were lost because of the collapse of a large financial institution.

It's been taking me some time to learn to understand what my dreams are trying to tell me. I started taking them more seriously when I failed to interpret one correctly in time! It was about pirates throwing people to the sharks. Shortly afterwards, the financial institution with whom I had my savings collapsed, so I lost my money. Afterwards I kicked myself for not having acted upon the warning, which now seemed so obvious!

Lee's dreams and contemplations had been giving her the same message for a long time, encouraging her towards her yearnings to work as a fine artist rather than as a commercial illustrator. In her waking life, her head told her she was untrained and should stay in her commercial career in order to continue earning something. Despite her dreams and the feelings of her heart and soul, Lee felt a lack of confidence in her ability to follow the artistic path

In preparation for a possible change, Lee started doing a few art classes here and there and felt she was building up to the right choice when 'The Mysterious Gift' arrived to give her the confidence she required to make the move a reality.

'The Mysterious Gift' was very convincing because my first husband was urging me to follow my own path. In real life I haven't had much support or encouragement from people close to me. They might think I've got the ability to do what I want but they're usually so involved in their own interests and problems that I come off second best. Most of the time my family and friends don't have the critical understanding or expertise to help me with my work.

My first husband was very helpful though, with art techniques in advertising, because we worked in the same area. In life he was sometimes enigmatic, with a clipped sense of humour, and could sound authoritarian, so his dream character was true to form in a more evolved sense. It seemed like now he was more in tune with my deeper needs and approved and encouraged them. There was a sense of urgency to get on with following my proper path, since he died quite young, at forty-one. The other thing which stood out in both dreams was the vividness of the paintings and the passion of the master. I woke up feeling exhilarated, like I could do that too, if I'd get over being so damned timid!

The overall effect was that Lee felt more settled that her choice of career change was right for her. There was a sense of confirmation and support from dream characters and art masters that was barely present in her waking life. 'The Mysterious Gift', once absorbed, was put into action:

I decided to stop doing commercial fashion art. The recession made this decision easier because it was in short supply and with regard to the designer mentioned, I was able to do less and less work for him as his daughter became more involved in the business. In the end I said no to further offers of work because I started to get involved in personal projects. I'm still only in the early stage of transition. It's very difficult because of the Pyramid Building Society collapse and the consequent loss of my savings. I haven't been able to get started again financially. There have also been family problems and lack of work space as our house is very small. So there is still a lot of sorting out to do.

Although Lee is feeling the financial pinch of branching out in a different direction and still has some amount of family matters to handle to help smooth her path, she is confident that her personal reasons for making this major change in her life will ultimately secure inner fulfilment.

I know that I have to do my own brand of creative work or I'll never be happy or at peace with myself. The worst part is that in order to do this I have gone onto unemployment benefits. It's tempting to try to find work in my old field but I know I'd just get on the treadmill again and resent it. Now that I'm getting older, the future in advertising or fashion isn't likely to be promising unless I have enough money to set up my own business. My intuition tells me this is the right time to make the change, though it will probably be a very slow, gradual process getting established in an alternative art career.

Meanwhile Lee's dreams continue to inspire her and light the way ahead, or warn her and prompt her into action whenever she moves away from her creativity.

If I have lapses where I don't attempt anything creative, I have very troubling dreams where I get attacked by a snake, usually biting my right hand. I'm sure it tries to wake me up and get me moving. My other interest is writing and I have similar dreams about pursuing this as a career too. I seem to be meant to pursue art and writing simultaneously but I don't know how to find enough time!

Lee's dreams continue to uncover the reasons why she tends to hold herself back, or lack confidence, while encouraging her to 'just do it'. It seems appropriate to finish her story with one of her own: another instalment from her inspirational dream life:

## A New Self 1993

I awaken with a flash of recognition. On the surface it may not look much, but I know I've just had a very important dream. I must sit up and take notice, recall every little detail — weigh its significance, then act upon it…

Pinpricks of bright colour like Aboriginal paintings dance and disperse before my eyes, making me feel inebriated. Something seems to come before me and replace me. I struggle to rise from my sick-bed which is little more than a mattress on the floor in communal living quarters of the kind I have come to know only too well since my children adopted alternative lifestyles — often invading my own space. My ability to move is restricted because I'm wearing my mother's heavy black serge coat with a tightly fitting belt and long flowing skirt — a stylish Dior look-alike from her heyday in the fifties. In the eighties I fished it out of her wardrobe and now my daughter borrows it too.

Suddenly my father appears, to help me. He hands me a large, light grey overcoat which is simple, practical, well-tailored and loose. It looks similar to Michel's (my second husband — I love to sneak my husband's coat from time to time). My father wants me to change into this new garment, which I do. The sensation of freedom makes me feel like flying! A vaguely familiar panorama opens before me: a vast green lawn with botanic gardens in the distance and pale blue sky above. The air smells fresh and fragrant, and carries the sound of bird-song. My father ushers me forward to be spirited across to the other side. In no time, we're approaching an impressive, modern, glass-fronted building with wide concrete steps leading to the entrance. It reminds me of the Union Hall at my old university. My father stops at the low colonnaded wall dividing the lawn from the pavement.

'Well, this is as far as I go,' he declares. Looking pensive, he adds 'I've been accused of holding you back. So, now it's up to you!'

I remember all the arguments and fights we used to have whenever I tried to follow either an artistic or academic course, and realise that this is his awkward way of saying 'Go with my blessing'. I hesitate, glancing back. I don't want to lose the sense of expansiveness. It makes me feel strong.

'Go on!,' he exhorts. 'Don't hang around admiring the view!'

Looking ahead, I spot my husband near the doorway of this substantial building. He smiles and my mind hears him pronounce 'Courage!' in the French manner that touches my soul. I hurry to greet him, pleased that he's there to offer support as I enter those portals to a new beginning.

I wake up knowing that it's time to do something I've always wanted to do. To go within and write.

## Jane's Interpretation

Lee's story, the result of combining two dreams, needs no interpretation. Apart from the obvious messages between all the quote marks, I love the way the painting of the poppy field becomes an actual garden of poppies which Lee chooses instead of the strange nourishment/medicine the advertising world was providing. The vision in the painter's eye became first a painting and then a living, breathing reality. We also have the power to create our personal reality.

Although Lee's story closely follows her original two dreams, an enlightening interpretation technique is to take several of your most prominent dream characters, settings and themes, combine them in some way, and write a fresh story or play about them. The idea is to let each character speak and interact with the other characters and settings, and then just let the plot develop on its own. It doesn't matter if the story or play goes off at a tangent to the dreams after a while. You will certainly learn something about yourself and your life in the process.

# Ocean Dip

## Heather – Jacaranda 1990

> The dream showed a far reaching view of mountains. Many trees softened the landscape and isolated lights from some houses on the hills added a feeling of comfort. A jacaranda tree emerged towards the centre of the dream.

My life at that time was devastating. I had reached an all-time emotional low and was under incredible stress. I had found myself caught in a situation where it was a case of either allow myself to be discredited, or tell the truth, which would have not only ruined two people, but their families would have suffered as a result.

Since it would never be an option for me to cause harm to anyone, let alone innocent people, I chose to remain quiet. I was aware that if I didn't move away, I wouldn't recover. To give myself a break from the trouble, I decided on a holiday at my son's property in the north.

From his house, there was an open view across the tops of mountains; many trees and a few scattered houses from which lights could be seen at night. I longed to stay there, but had to return to my home down south. My concern for a grandchild was such that returning seemed the only thing I could do.

The dream showed me a profound peace of mind that I had forgotten existed. Once experienced, it became like a magnet, drawing me towards the direction in which the dream, and its location, pointed.

I decided to return to live in the north. It took only a month between the dream and making the move, and I settled in a pretty rural town that I had liked while on holiday. This was a severe wrench for me, as I worried about my grandson. My health continued to deteriorate and a succession of dreams reassured me that my grandson received much spiritual protection, so I found the courage to go forward in my own interest.

The jacaranda tree from the dream belonged to a family whom I met soon after arriving up north. It was several months before we realised that our paths had crossed some twenty-five to twenty-six years before we met. The husband was shocked when he realised who I was. He said No-one should have to suffer what was done to you at the time', referring to a bad marriage and deception over property and money. His family was highly respected in the district. I was accepted because of my association with them.

I have no regrets at taking action on my dream. The four years since making the move have been difficult at times, due to several stress-related illnesses. Nevertheless, a pattern of positive influences began to emerge. I have now reached the stage where my health is much better, except for my vision, which has been irreparably damaged. I am happy and have many friends, some from the past who remained loyal, and I enjoy peace of mind.

## Jane's Interpretation

Just as a landscape painting captures a mood, an outlook, a juxtaposition of foreground to background, a central focus and a distant view, the dreamscape (the dream's landscape) carries the same potential for interpretation. Our dreamscapes may capture our present mood, present outlook and present focal point, summarising our subconscious assessment of our present life in one grand picture. Alternatively our dreamscapes may paint pictures to inspire or motivate ourselves towards a higher goal or purpose. Novice dream interpreters frequently find this confusing. How can we tell which dreams enlighten us, or put us in the picture about our present situation, and which entice us to make positive, life-enhancing changes? When the subconscious speaks, it often does so without reference to time.

The answer is easy: ask the dreamer! The dreamer knows whether the dreamscape corresponds to his or her present situation, or whether it represents an enticement to move forward. The dreamer's response is unlikely to be a vague 'I suppose so', as if they are trying to fit the interpretation to their life or their wishes. When the interpretation matches either the dreamer's present condition or a feasible future, he or she will feel a definite 'yes, that's it!' as the interpretation resonates with the subconscious.

In Heather's case, the feeling of peace, a complete contrast to her state of mind at the time of the dream, inspired and motivated her to move into a similar environment, as her story tells. The appearance of the jacaranda tree in her waking life acted as a synchronicity to confirm the importance of the dream, the necessity to place herself in a peaceful environment.

Knowing Heather's dreamscape was futuristic, the interpretation becomes a portrayal of the gains Heather's subconscious was seeking in inspiring her to look for more peace in her life. The tree emerging towards the centre of

Heather's dream probably represents herself, the central character in her own dreamscape. The fact that she, or the tree, is placed centrally is a good sign: well centred, focused. Presumably the tree was seen as healthy. Heather would need to ask herself 'If a jacaranda tree had a personality, what would it be?', to get a more accurate picture of the personal benefits of the move. She would also be wise to contemplate what other significance jacaranda trees might have in her life, as this may be the central issue requiring her attention in a peaceful setting.

The rest of the view is panoramic and the feelings the dreamscape inspires are the interpretation: comfort, softened and far reaching. This is what she needed most at the time of the dream, and this is what she decided to go out and make happen in her life.

# Ocean Dip

## Mary – A Change of Scene 1986

I was going to work in the city in my car. The streets were dark and deserted. I parked and walked to the place where I was to work. It was a deserted building, no-one was there.

I knew I was to operate a computer in a darkened room alone and I worked for some time. A man came into the room and told me I had worked beyond my shift. I told him that I might as well stay and do the next shift. When I left I was not able to find my car.

I walked alone through dark, deserted streets, anxious, fearful and lonely. Suddenly I was high on a hill in dazzling sunlight. A wide open road lay before me: it was deserted. I knew I was expected to walk down that road, but I was afraid to do so because I was concerned that fast cars might come along and hit me. A child appeared and was starting to walk down the road but I stopped the child from going because I feared for its safety.

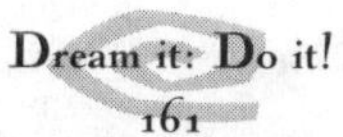

This dream came very soon after a break-up of a long-term relationship with a man I presumed I'd marry. I was stunned and very depressed, although I had initiated it.

The dream left a big impression, largely because the change of scene was so dramatic from dark, narrow, twisted streets to brilliant light and a wide open road which was actually shining. My mood was changed in an instant from one of depression to one of elation and excitement.

I had been reading a lot on dreams and their meanings and interpreted the dream as follows: I had lost direction. My life was going nowhere and I was lonely and unhappy. I had lost count of time and had devalued myself to the extent that I was willing to work longer hours in inhuman conditions like an automaton. In the depths of despair a new path opened up, if only I would choose to walk down it. Part of me was eager to take the chance but I was aware that I needed to take time to be sure the way was safe to travel. I'd been badly hurt and needed nurturing, and not risk making decisions too soon, but the chance was there when I was ready.

A series of dreams reinforced the message from that first one. I wasn't aware of taking any steps at that time to turn my life around other than becoming more involved in my career, working on my self-esteem and just getting through, but I began seeing results of the changes I was making in my life after about a year. Looking back, I realise now how my self-esteem and confidence have increased one hundred per cent since the day I had that dream years ago.

My life is very different now. Eventually, after some years apart and no contact, I met the man again. We had both changed so much, gained in maturity, self-esteem and confidence. We married; now we are very happy.

## Jane's Interpretation

My interpretation would have been very similar to Mary's. Mary makes the point that further dreams reinforced her conclusions about the meaning of this dream. This is the built-in 'safety device' we can always rely on. If you interpret a dream and it recurs without change, then you have probably either misinterpreted or not taken action. The dream repeats itself because the issue it concerns has not been addressed in waking life. The secret is to interpret a dream and take a tentative step towards action — a very small, safely-tested step. If your interpretation is correct, further dreams will slap you on the back in congratulation at the move you have made and encourage you to go further. If you misinterpreted your dream, though, following dreams will certainly hold up big 'STOP!' signs. This should not be taken as an indication of inadequacy in dream interpretation, but as a positive sign to go back to the drawing board because, knowing what the dream does NOT mean is a big step towards elucidating what it DOES mean. This 'trial and error' approach can be very successful, but remember, it only works when you take small testing steps on your interpretation first!

There may also have been a warning in Mary's dream that her natural tendency would be to work on herself in isolation, or to stay in 'deserted' mode to address her relationship breakdown, rather than to begin the journey and tackle the fears. While this might be a suitable method of working through grief for some people, Mary's dream suggested that lingering too long, 'beyond the call of duty', might result in losing her direction or drive (symbolised by losing her car) altogether. Perhaps the dream showed a solution to this natural dilemma. Mary realised through the dream that a light-filled path did exist, that there was direction in her life and that it was there for the taking when, and only when, she felt nurtured and resilient enough to face any risks that new journey might involve.

Dream scenes often change dramatically from night to brilliant sun-filled day when we bring insight from the (dark, unknown) subconscious into the clearly seen light of the conscious mind. In Mary's case, the newfound conscious knowledge was that a future direction did exist, that there were fears to overcome, and that her best approach would be a gentle one.

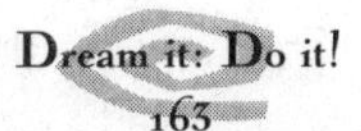

Realising potential by getting into the driver's seat and taking back control in life was a major factor in the life-changing dreams of seven people: Mell, Akira, Dee Dee, Nellie, Kate, Andy and Michaela.

Michaela, as we will see, did it literally in her dream, grabbing the wheel from the back seat and reclaiming her rightful place as captain of her own destiny.

## Ocean Dip

## Michaela – Michaela's Dream 1985

> I was a small child in the back of my father's car. The car was all over the road and I was being thrown around all over the place. I felt very frightened. All of a sudden I looked at my father's face. It seemed so ugly and horrible.
>
> With a surge of courage and determination I reached across the seat, leaned over his shoulders and straightened up the steering wheel and took control of the car. The car started to drive in a straight line forward.

My life before this was a life of anxiety, fear, distrust and panic.

I came from a dysfunctional family and my father was very angry and sometimes violent. I was a victim of physical, mental and emotional abuse, but, thankfully, not sexual abuse. Being so young, and not having the emotional strength to endure this situation, I repressed my feelings and pain. I put a smile on my face and totally blocked off my feelings.

My father died when I was twenty-five years old. By this time I was married to a lovely man and had four children. I had everything a person could want but I was unhappy at times. I needed to look inside and heal my pain. By the time I was twenty-nine years old my body had totally broken down. I needed help but I did not know where to go.

This dream was the turning point. I interpreted it as meaning that my father had instilled so much fear in me as a child that I was still letting this control my life as an adult. I could let myself go downhill even more, or I had the power to make changes in my life. It was time for me to take control of my destiny. I acted on the dream immediately and my life path has been straight and onward forward since.

I took control of my life and released the pain that held me back. I achieved this by a process of looking inside through meditation which released all the hurt, and through reading books on spirituality. This gave me hope and faith. At thirty-three years of age I began to have spiritual healing. After about six months of continuous visits to the healing centre I began to feel well again.

I have perfect health now. I feel I have totally forgiven, accepted and released my father. I have thanked him for the experience. This life with my family and parents has not only made me a stronger person but I now help others to heal by spiritual healing, counselling and other natural modalities. I have a meditation group each week also. I feel my creativity has awakened and that I am full, like a rose in bloom.

## Jane's Interpretation

Michaela's dream clearly illustrates the power of a personality, even after death, to control the life of another. Yet this is not the full story. As Michaela realised, what we perceive as being controlled by another person is often more a case of allowing ourselves to be subject to their control. Even after death. In any relationship we tend to accept and reject aspects of another's personality, changing the way we are. We learn from the relationship and adapt accordingly. We admire and assimilate traits of the other, become convinced by them and take on their perceptions, or recoil and develop in opposition to everything they represent. We respond to the other with delight, fear, love, denial, indeed a whole barrage of emotions, conditioning ourselves into set behaviour patterns, attitudes and perceptions which we take forward to weave into our future relationships. As children, of course, we are especially vulnerable in our relationships with our parents. Dreams such as Michaela's help us to see ourselves in perspective and to see which aspects of our early conditioning are inappropriate in our adult lives.

Car dreams are excellent metaphors for the way we move through our life. Cars can represent our drive (literally), our motivation (is the engine working well?), our energy levels (fuel?), our progress (going forward, slipping back or stuck in the mud?), our style (what kind of car?), our direction (where are we going, or are we lost?), how difficult we perceive our journey to be (any vertical roads to negotiate?) and much more. Dreams of realising you are not in control of your own life (not at the wheel, not feeling in control, or worse still, like Michaela, both) have the power to shock us into firmly grabbing that steering wheel once and for all.

## River 19

## Mell – The Riverwall Dream 1992

It is night, a lovely peaceful, moonlit night, and my husband and I are lying in bed. It seems we have moved to a new house and the bedroom is unfamiliar and mysterious to me, but I sense that I am going to like it very much.

One long wall (the outside wall) is missing, so although the structure is normal in all other respects, I have a strong feeling of oneness with the night and the outside world. Right at the edge of the room — where the bed is set parallel to the missing wall and I am lying looking out into the peaceful darkness — a river laps gently, flowing parallel to the missing wall. I could almost reach out a hand and touch the water.

For a moment I'm a little concerned about this and say to my husband 'But what if it floods? We'll drown in our sleep and everything will be washed away and ruined'.

He tells me very calmly that no, this won't happen. Everything is perfectly safe and exactly as it should be. The river will always stay like this, and just to relax and enjoy it with total trust and confidence.

There is a second scene to the dream, following on immediately: another part of the same unfamiliar house, and I am standing in the dining room, facing into the lounge. The entire front wall of the house is made of unpainted grey besser-blocks, as if it has been deliberately walled up. There are no windows, no doors, and no light can get through from the outside or even any fresh air.

A feeling of panic overwhelms me. I can't live here. I can't survive like this. I feel trapped, a sensation like being buried alive.

I say to my husband, who appears to be waiting for my verdict, 'No!, I hate it! I can't stay here even a moment longer'.

He reaches out towards the wall and shows me a miracle. 'See?' he says. 'It's all in your mind. If you don't like it this way, you can make it better any time you decide. It's up to you.'

Suddenly the wall is a yellow and orange curtain, sliding sideways, and all at once the whole room is flooded with sunlight. Finally I understand with blinding clarity that it is all up to me. As soon as I make up my mind to do it, I can free myself — pull open the curtain, see outside, go out into freedom if I want. I'm the creator of my own prison. It's only real because I've chosen to believe that it is. The miracle is — it doesn't have to be that way at all!

For a long time, maybe six or seven years, I had been steadily 'losing it'. Looking back, I realise now that a kind of emotional damming up had been going on in me since childhood. A lot of stuff had happened back then which I had absorbed but had never let myself deal with or even acknowledge was taking place. The best way I can describe it is as feeling, all my life, of having been a sort of cripple.

I knew something was very badly wrong with me, or missing, but for some reason I was able to hide it from other people. I was

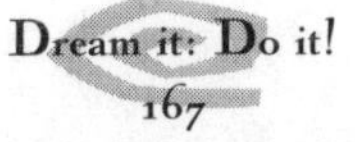

very good at pretending. It was hard, at times very nearly impossible to sustain, yet through childhood and into early adulthood I managed pretty well. I had a few weird phobias: for one thing, I couldn't eat or drink if anyone else was around. Yet somehow I led a fairly normal life.

Then, in my early thirties, little things started coming unglued. Before long panic attacks were becoming a major problem. I got to the point where any sort of social occasion was torture. People terrified me. I felt vulnerable and threatened and irrationally panicked at the idea of even meeting an acquaintance in the street and having to speak to him or her. In the end I stopped going anywhere, except to those few things that were impossible to avoid.

The world seemed to be shutting down, doors slamming closed, locking me into a smaller and smaller space. There was so much I longed to do, things to learn, things to share, yet I felt I was shrinking and moving further and further away from everything.

Marie, my closest friend, realised what was happening, and my husband did too. They both tried to talk some sense into me but nothing really seemed to make any difference. I'd lost control and no matter how hard I tried, I couldn't get back in the driver's seat.

The situation kept worsening as time went by. As you can imagine, this was a horrible period. I became pretty desperate, and think eventually I was almost ready to stop even thinking about turning 'normal' again, when the dream came. Melodramatic as it may sound, I credit this one dream with actually saving my life!

The impact of the dream was indescribable. There was no need to ponder or interpret symbols, the meaning was clear. The dream made me see the whole situation for what it was, in a way which made instantaneous and total sense. The realisation that nothing external was responsible for my situation, that the whole cause and solution rested with me, was comparable to a bolt of lightening.

Basically, I realised what I was fighting was myself. And fighting was not the way to go about the problem at all. I had to accept. It was OK to be me. It was OK to be a little weird. Who wasn't? Did I expect perfection from other people? No. So, why punish myself to the point of annihilation because I wasn't either?

The change began immediately. In effect, what I did was give myself permission to be. The steps were small and painfully slow, but gradually the momentum picked up. I'm so much easier with myself now. It's strange to imagine how things could have become so horrific. I still have setbacks; I still get very shaky and sometimes have to withdraw a bit from people to take a breather, but on the whole I'd say I'm about eighty per cent functional.

Jane, coming to see you lecture that night was a big achievement for me. Sitting there, feeling all those people so close, and not letting panic take hold was really something. At the interval it would have been nice to walk up and say hello to you, but being out in public and actually *speaking* was more than I could have managed in one night at that time.

POSTSCRIPT

Panic attacks have a way of wearing a person down, mentally and physically. Energies and the ability to cope from day to day get drained to the limit. I realise now I that I was unusually accident-prone before the dream, when things were really bad. I can think of several incidents, in particular, and all of them were injuries to my legs, ankles, feet, etc.

Having since read a bit of what Louise Hayes has to say about problems related to various parts of the body — well, it makes you wonder!

## Jane's Interpretation

Dream houses (houses which do not exist in our waking world) usually symbolise the dreamer's state of mind. Each room in the house reflects compartments of thought, the kitchen, for example, perhaps symbolising nourishment and nurturing, and the bathroom representing a place of (emotional) cleansing. Since our physical health and wellbeing generally relates to mental attitude (mental stress, for example, being a major contributor to physical disease), the dream house can also be seen as symbolic of the dreamer's physical health.

Mell experiments with knocking down one of the solid walls she has built in her mind. With the wall gone, she can almost touch the flow of life (the river) outside. For a moment she fears that contact with the outer world will prove too emotional an experience for her (the flooding river which could drown her). She then relaxes and feels safe in the dark, secure in the mystery, comfortable with trusting herself to be more open and allowing herself to flow, like the river, with life. Her husband supports her through this gentle experiment of making contact with the outside world. Although he presents as her husband in the dream, he is probably symbolic of her 'inner male' (Yang qualities of assertiveness, logic, intellectual self and general relationship with the outer world). In her waking life, at that time, Mell drew little strength from her inner male, but this dream contact enabled her to feel the security 'he' could offer her. If she wished to do so, she could tap into her own inner strength for support in facing the outer world at any time.

In the second scene she clearly sees the walls she has built in her mind: they are grey, the colour of depression and lack of life. There are no windows (no view or open perspective on the world), no doors (no opportunities opening up, no prospects entering into her life), and no light (no conscious development, no joy). She realises she has created this, that she has mentally buried herself alive. How beautifully the sun suddenly explodes into the room as she reports 'finally I understand with blinding clarity'. The full light of consciousness has burst upon her as she realises she, and no-one or nothing else, has always been the author of her own life.

# Ocean Dip

## Wendy – Babies 1980-90

A long series of dreams always required me to mind someone else's baby which had to be breast fed. I would put it aside with every good intention of doing the best for it. With horror I would remember it hours or days later. I'd run to it, thinking it was most likely dead. I'd always arrive just in time. Each dream presented different situations but with the same results.

In the last one of the series, I put twins in their carry baskets in a ground floor wardrobe, on the floor, whilst I was upstairs busily doing other things. It was about a week later that I remembered them. Totally devastated, I raced downstairs just in time to save them. I had been sure they would be dead.

I was always doing more for others, and particularly being a lone parent, for my children. The dreams always had an upsetting effect: it was terrible being responsible for almost killing a baby through neglect, but twins were the utter limit! It took this last dream to really work it out.

Finally I realised the babies were me. I was all the time giving to others and totally neglecting myself. After all those recurring dreams, the twins caused me to take action within a matter of only days. It was time to give more to myself, and I set out to do this.

Sometimes, when feeling overly imposed upon or not considered, I pause, reflect on my position, then set about regaining a balance. I feel so relieved and much freer and happier now.

### Jane's Interpretation

Babies often symbolise the part of ourselves we should be nurturing and caring for, but which we so often overlook in focusing on the needs of others, or in putting too much emphasis on some of our personal needs while neglecting other important areas. Babies can also represent our 'baby

projects', the ideas we are developing, the creativity or careers we are nurturing, and so on. Wendy's final dream beautifully illustrates the way in which a dream goes for added impact by magnifying or duplicating the vital dream symbol: the single baby became twins!

Babies are excellent dream symbols, since most people respond to the vulnerability of a tiny baby. What we have difficulty with is transferring the same amount of care to ourselves. One way of achieving this is to find a photo of yourself as a tiny baby, frame it and keep it in prominent view for a while. Examine it closely and build up a mental picture of how you looked, how you might have moved, laughed and cried. Do this until you can close your eyes and picture your baby self clearly, feel the warmth of your body and sense the baby smell of your skin. Then, for a week or so, imagine you are carrying this baby everywhere with you: even on a trip to the bathroom. For those few weeks, each time you have to make a decision, consider what you would decide for the baby. It is much easier to do something kind and nurturing for your baby self than it is to do the same thing for yourself. In time you learn to care for yourself while eradicating the feeling that such self-attention is selfish.

## River 20

## Andy – The Winds of Change 1994

On the other side of the stream the grass wavered up to the base of some tall trees and many miles in the distance behind the trees was a mountain range which ran up to a huge snow-capped peak. A thin wisp of cirrus cloud hung overhead and I watched as the wind raced up the right-hand side of the peak and blew the snow and ice off the top: an incredible sight. Turning back to see what the others were doing I noticed the position of the sun and how warm it was. I could smell the snow…

Deb walked down the hill between her boyfriend and the Maori (all were in their sleeping bags). She came up behind me and, to my delight, lay down, put her arms around me and cuddled into my back. I looked over my shoulders and she was looking at me, smiling. I turned back around, smiling too and feeling content. She did what I was hoping she would do.

A few seconds later we began to slide headfirst down the hill. I couldn't move my arms or legs as the sleeping bag was tied up around my neck. Deb held her arms tightly around my waist. I could feel the moisture from grass spears dripping down my face. We stopped at the bottom of the hill and lay there, laughing. I removed the sleeping bag as Deb slowly rose to her feet.

She put her left hand up, the back of her hand facing me and wiggled her fingers. 'I've lost my ring,' she said. 'We have to find it.'

In the centre of a small gorge lay a large, flat rock, diamond-shaped. The stream ran down through the gorge then split and flowed either side of this rock. Deb removed her top and lay on the stone, feeling the warmth of the sun, while I searched some more for the ring. At the foot of this stone was a small pool where the stream re-joined after flowing around the stone. I took off my shoes and walked over to it, feeling the icy alpine water which was crystal clear to look into. I searched for Deb's ring in the pool below her feet. On the bottom of the pool lay small pebbles of different colours, shapes and sizes, all smooth and rounded. I pulled out one small pebble: it was light green, like jade, and had a distinct small notch in the top. It had been worn smooth over the years by running water and sand.

I held this stone for quite some time. I rubbed it, turned it over, and watched the sun glisten on it when I held it up. At that moment there was a mental thought, a message in a girl's voice, saying 'Give it to Deb, ...'

When I turned around, things had changed. I was looking at a beautiful snow scene. In front of me were glistening smooth boulders, about two feet high and all strewn around an area of about twenty square feet. Behind them were pine trees, all heavily laden with pure white snow. The boulders were covered in beautiful mosses and lichens of greens, greys and reds. I was still

looking for the ring, now among the lichen. It was rough, but not difficult to pull back. I could feel a rumbling under my feet and could hear the sound of running water…

I came to a gorge, about sixty feet deep and eighty feet across, where a huge, powerful, rumbling waterfall of snow and water poured down. On the other side of the gorge was the most magnificent alpine forest running up to the base of another huge mountain, this time only a mile or so away. Again I watched the wind blow the snow off the peak and swirl it around.

I stood with a feeling of contentment, at one with myself and what was around me. I was alone standing there. No-one else anywhere was witnessing what I was. I could feel the cool refreshing spray and mist on my face as it came up the side of the gorge…

Admiring the lichen, something else caught my eye. Two young deer were watching me: a young stag with small velvet covered stumps on his head, the beginnings of antlers, and a smaller doe. We watched each other for a few moments. The stag made a move towards me, just a couple of steps, put his head out towards me, sniffed the air, then stepped back to the female. They walked towards me side by side, not frightened by my presence at all. They danced off over the boulders and disappeared under a pine, knocking the snow off a lower branch as they passed.

I stood reflecting for a moment and was about to turn to leave when I was hit in the face by a snowball: it was Deb and she looked beautiful. We felt happy to be together, joked about something and began to ski off. I was first: I had no skis, only boots!

Andy's dream, as he wrote it down the next morning, was twelve foolscap pages long. The above is a series of excerpts, necessarily edited for inclusion in this book.

I have had vivid dreams in the past but none more than this. The clarity and 'realness' was incredible. I can remember this dream more clearly than I can remember a recent trip to Sydney. Although it was not lucid, there was nothing in the dream to indicate it was a dream. There was nothing bizarre. Nothing strange or surreal occurred. In short, nothing out of the ordinary at all happened. And that is exactly what really stood out. It was, and I can't say it any clearer, 'too real'. When I woke up it took me a few moments to realise it was a dream. I lay in bed thinking I had just come back from holiday; and, in a sense, I had. All my senses were very much alive and throughout the dream I was very clear-headed. I knew what I was saying, doing, thinking and feeling, but I did not know it was a dream, not for one second.

Three days after the dream, while walking to the beach with my flatmate, Phil, we came across a large, blue-green jellyfish which had been broken up by kids. I noticed something in amongst the broken jelly: it was a shape that caught my eye. The dream came back to me straight away as I picked up a small piece of blue-green glass, worn smooth over the years from water and sand. Its shape, dimensions, weight, everything was exactly as the pebble appeared in the dream. For a couple of days I rubbed this piece of glass over and over in my hand, looked at it from every angle and held it up to the light. I knew I had given this to Deb in the dream, but what it meant I had no idea. A friend suggested I make it into a necklace and send it to her, which I have done.

Before the dream Andy, a builder, had fallen in love with Deb who said she felt the same way. On a working trip overseas, however, she fell in love with someone else and wrote to tell Andy that their relationship was over. This happened within a matter of a week, which left Andy feeling devastated.

It was the discovery of the glass stone from my dream on the beach the next day which made me contact Jane Anderson after finding her book, *Sleep On It and Change Your Life*, in the local bookstore. I had no idea what it meant other than it was to be looked further into.

The dream interpretation was involved and almost as lengthy as Andy's original twelve-page dream! It included a look back into Andy's emotional past, a comparison to his state at the time of the dream, and a glimpse ahead to the potential of his future. Although he skied off with Deb at the end of the dream, she was symbolic of his 'female' side, his Yin, indicating the potential not for the relationship to be reinstated, but for Andy's future achievements once he came to terms with his whole self (including his Yin): just look at the ease with which he happily skied off, not even requiring the skis!

The terrific landscapes revealed Andy's emotional landscapes at various points in his life and development and there were many 'turn arounds' or 'looking backs' to emphasise the insights, the glimpses of the past, or the changes in his life. Snow, being frozen water, tends to represent frozen emotions, so there was much recognition of old frozen emotions and consequent thawing and melting. Andy's relationship with Deb melted snow, the deer (aspects of himself) brushed off more in recognition of the importance of walking on without fear. The winds (of change, or the breaths of fresh air) whipped away the hardest icy snow from the very mountain tops.

In digging for the ring, the symbol of unity between Andy and his 'female' side (like an engagement ring?), he was searching and digging to find his own personal riches. The dream commented throughout on how to find this unity within himself. He dug deep into the lichen, where the snow had been thawed, close to the earth below which lay his subconscious where more needed to be revealed. Deep within he heard the mighty rumble of water and later saw the waterfall, resplendently releasing chunks of snow as it spouted out into the gorge. And so Andy was realising the power that digging deep could achieve: the release and spewing out of old frozen emotions.

Unity he did achieve, not only at the end of the dream, but also in his moment of contentment, being at one with himself on the edge of the gorge. It all certainly hit him in the face, just as Deb's snowball represented her own coolness and frozen emotions that she hurled at him when she found herself a new boyfriend. Even so, they laughed, because Andy realised, in his dream state, that she had given him the greatest gift of all. In her hardness towards him he was challenged to the depths of his subconscious to work out why this had happened and how he could use this information about himself to better his future.

Perhaps the stone represented a 'karmic debt', something Andy repaid to Deb. Whatever it was, it was a synchronicity, and its major importance was that it reappeared on the beach in Andy's waking life to beg the question of the meaning of his dream and to spur him into taking steps towards self-discovery.

My subconscious was taking me very carefully through my past, present and, upon the synchronicity, my future. It was impossible not to look and act upon this dream; as Jane Anderson wrote in her book, 'a synchronicity is there, in your waking life, screaming at you to find an answer'. If she hadn't worked that out for me I'd probably be walking around in one of those jackets with the eight foot wrap-around sleeves!

The emotions which I had kept on ice for the last five years melted as a direct result of my relationship with Deb. The stone was indeed a 'karmic debt' which has finally been repaid. It was a debt to a girl, Naomi, who I was with before Deb. I had been deeply hurt when I found out that my long-time girlfriend before Naomi had been having an affair with a good friend of mine, so I closed myself away for three years. She tried in vain to help me to let go of the hurt and the repressed emotions and she suffered terribly mentally and finally left. Realising what I had done, I let go. For a year and a half after that I felt guilt for what she went through.

Along came Deb and within a couple of days she had not only stolen my heart but had also told me that every boyfriend she'd ever had had treated her like dirt and put her down. Subconsciously I picked up on this and gave her more love, respect, appreciation and affection than anyone ever had. She would cry frequently about it because she was so overwhelmed. What I was doing, in fact, was paying back Naomi, the previous girlfriend. Deb has since been very spiteful, selfish and ungrateful and I now see her as the person I used to be. She represses her emotions from the past.

So how did Andy use what he had learned to change his life?

After receiving this interpretation I began looking more and more at my dreams, very much self-discovery, personal growth and awareness sort of stuff. With a lot of soul searching I began to realise I was not using my full potential. I had to take a look ahead and see not just what I had to do, but more of what I wanted to do. To be able to do this I had to look deeply and face a few home truths. I had to find my confidence and self-esteem and discover why I was lacking in this area. This mental flush out and consequent cleansing went for about two months. After that, for another month, my dreams took on a different form, very positive, one after another. I was killed a few times, which to me is a good sign: out with the old, on with the new. Dream doors started to fly open in front of me without me even touching them, like something out of a Schwartznegger movie: it was hilarious!

I took up horse riding. In the past I had no confidence and had been scared of this huge beast made of muscle under me. I had a large quarter horse, a very powerful beast, and jumped in so full of confidence that in ten minutes we were trotting, something I never thought I was capable of. In half an hour we were on the beach at sunset at full gallop. I have never felt so free. On the way home my horse shied terribly at a car. He went sideways into the road and spun around. In a few seconds I had him under control and back off the road. My friend just stared at me in disbelief and said 'That was amazing, you are so well balanced!' I knew what she meant, but I received it in a different way. In a few seconds I thought of the dream, the stone, my past, my future and my present mental and emotional state and I laughed all the way home.

At this time I was looking deeper and deeper into my dreams, asking questions and receiving answers, facing fears and overcoming them, albeit sometimes in a pretty bizarre manner, as some of my dreams are pretty outrageous. At the end of the third month I made my decision to take on university and study counselling and mediation.

The steps I have taken are in the right direction. I now have a major goal to achieve. I have no fears and I am confident that I can accomplish the course I will be undertaking.

Looking back on the changes in my life, the first dream made me 'look', the synchronicity made me 'realise', and my following dreams made me 'take charge'.

### Jane's Interpretation

Since Andy consulted me shortly after he had this dream, my interpretation is already included in the account.

## River 21

## Akira – Where am I? 1990

> Looking at myself in the mirror I was unable to see my image. I remember the feeling of panic as I was rubbing the mirror with my hand trying to clean it and yet still I could not see my image. I knew there was something desperately wrong and I just didn't know what to do.

I felt that I had lost control over my life. I was tired, losing weight, felt stressed and was confused. I felt that I was here for a special purpose, but that I was not fulfilling this purpose. I was beginning to feel a victim of life.

I was becoming more and more reclusive and had put my family on hold, as I always put Simon's wishes before my own. I didn't know how it had all happened but I was losing my identity, my individuality, and I was living my life through Simon, in his shadow so to speak. I was aware that I had allowed this situation to develop, but I felt powerless to change anything.

I had a number of dreams similar to my mirror dream during early 1990. I think there may have been two of these. In the first one my image was a little clearer and in the second one, it faded altogether. These dreams signalled a turning point in my life.

The dreams were straightforward to Akira, and needed little interpretation. Quite simply:

My image, my form, was literally fading away. The dream left me feeling so shocked that I knew I absolutely had to take action. I guess I knew that I would leave my body soon if I did nothing. Although I am not afraid of dying, I knew that I had work to do that I had not completed, even though at this stage I didn't fully understand my purpose here.

I had always been into natural therapies and had a lot of success in connecting to my higher self and greater wisdom through the use of flower essences and gem therapy. I wrote to a friend, a flower essence practitioner, in whom I had confided for a time and who had made up a number of flower and gem remedies for me in the past. He sent me yet another remedy. This time my greater attunement, as a result of this, led me to a naturopath who had recently moved into my area. I made an appointment for a massage.

During the course of the massage, my newly found friend tuned into my body and discovered that I had lost most of my muscle tone, that I had a serious pancreatic enzyme deficiency, and later told me that she had felt I was just a few days away from leaving my body. Because of my enzyme deficiency I had been digesting only about a quarter of my food intake.

I spent the next several months seeing her on a regular basis. Over the next two years or so I gradually built myself up again, with proper food combining, herbal and mineral supplements, digestive enzymes, exercise and so on.

These changes were actually the result of a series of dreams. Following on from the 'mirror dreams' I received many dreams of guidance in how to deal with my day-to-day situation and interactions with others. Foods I needed to eat, supplements I needed to take, gemstones to use, flower essences to take, and so on, all came in dreams.

As my body became stronger, gradually my mental and emotional strength grew as well. I began to take greater control of my life, but this took quite a long time. Eventually I left Simon, as I felt I just could not really be myself so long as I stayed with him.

I travelled and had never felt quite so free. It was the first time in my life since I was a teenager that I had not been in a relationship. There was just me and I realised that life was exciting and that I could do whatever I liked!

I dreamt about Mexico, and Chichen Itza and the Yucatan Peninsula, and I knew that one day I needed to go there and connect with that energy. This I did during the time Simon and I were apart. I felt that during this trip I connected to and released a lot of past life stuff and connected to a lot of wisdom in Mexico.

In time I returned to Simon, who had needed the break as much as I did to review his life and decide what he really wanted. This time it's different.

I had a dream, early in 1991, that we had decided to go to Fiji for a holiday. So we did, and I realised when we were there that there was a lot more to this holiday than I had first realised. I knew that connecting to the energy of that place was for the purpose of bringing into our conscious awareness 'stuff' that was deeply repressed and needed to be dealt with. Over the next year or so, as a result of this holiday, a number of personal issues were dealt with. Sometimes I see the old patterns creeping in, but I am more aware and can mostly deal with the energy before any uncomfortable life situations manifest themselves.

My only regret is that it took me so long to take many of the actions that followed the dream. My final action in taking my own space and travelling was absolutely one of the best I have taken in my life. During that time, I always had the love and support of my family and we became close again during this time I was on my own. I met and made some wonderful friends, I developed more confidence in myself and felt more self-worth than I had in years. And my health was great, too!

I see my family when it feels right, taking space when I need it. I am much more in control. Back with Simon I am now much stronger and know that I am fine, on my own or in partnership.

### Jane's Interpretation

What we see in dream mirrors can be quite enlightening. We think we know who we are until we see ourselves reflected back, looking quite different. A mirror enables us to look at ourselves more objectively, and although waking life mirrors can lie, and we are clever at seeing what we want to see, or of focusing on the negative, our dream mirrors tend to reflect a more honest, if symbolic, picture. In dreams we truly see ourselves because the subconscious deals in home truths. If you see a mirror in a dream, gather courage and have a look!

Akira's image had disappeared. She saw herself as fading away, losing her identity. No-one was there. She acknowledged in the dream, perhaps for the first time, that something was desperately wrong, but the dream also showed her that she had lost control over her life because she no longer knew what to do. Awareness is always the first step. Once awareness of a problem is transferred to waking life consciousness, further dreams usually reveal the necessary direction and guidance. Acceptance or acknowledgement prepares us to take successful action. We need to know where we are before we can measure the next step.

## Ocean Dip

## Dee Dee – Courage 1987

Everybody was telling me what I should do, what I shouldn't to do and what I was supposed to say to different people. I told them to get off my back and leave me alone.

My marriage was full of arguments and rows all the time, so I interpreted the dream as meaning I had to stand up for myself and not let my husband do all the decision-making for me. It took six months to put the dream into action, but it changed my life.

In the dream I had the courage to tell people to get off my back, so I finally told my husband that there would be no more arguments or rows, and that I could make my own decisions for myself. I asked him to let me do so. Everything just seemed to fall into place after that.

Dee Dee's dreams came to her rescue again in 1994, encouraging her to make a further important stand:

> I dreamed I was on a deserted island which was being flooded by sea water. I could not get off the island no matter how I tried. I was stuck there.

At the time of the dream I had been wearing myself into the ground with fundraising and helping out at the school. I was having bad migraines and the dream feeling of being flooded by sea water was an image of my life. I felt the dream was warning me that if I did not slow down with what I was doing, my life or my world was going to collapse or cave in on me.

I decided to slow down before I burnt out, so two months later I stopped helping out at the school. Although I regret upsetting my youngest son very much because of this, I feel quite happy with my action.

## Jane's Interpretation

The power of role-playing in a dream pays off again. All Dee Dee had to do was identify the situation she needed to stand up to in her waking life, and then do it!

# River 22

## Kate – Trusting the Process 1994

I dreamed a friend came to my home with a bottle of champagne. It was as though our previous disagreement had not happened. She embraced me and I told her that I loved her. We had the champagne.

In a similar dream another friend entered carrying a bottle of champagne, which she opened and poured. She asked me if I wanted some. I refused, saying I'd stick to the cask of white wine I had in the fridge. I placed the cask on the table. Then I noticed she had on the table two bottles of champagne wrapped up with cellophane with cards and ribbons. She said they were for me. I felt very grateful about this, but I had the feeling I just couldn't take her champagne.

I had started to have problems with some really close girlfriends; two separate instances, in fact. After the first girlfriend and I clashed, violently, many things were said in the heat of the moment. My friend, I realised, was carrying around a lot of 'shit'. She was threatened with bankruptcy and I was very close to the situation, going to court on her behalf and taking on her problems, as well as my own. Exactly one week later, after no contact, I had the first champagne dream. Another week passed and I received something through the mail which I'd been waiting on from her, so I rang her to thank her and it was as though nothing had happened. Our relationship is now very healthy and we have never mentioned the incident to each other.

The attitude of unconditional acceptance and understanding which the dream had inspired gave Kate the opportunity to see her friendship in a new light and handle it differently. When the second friendship was challenged, it was Kate who required the unconditional support.

On the second occasion I had become very drunk at a function with a friend. I may drink at home, but for some reason on this occasion, I did it outside, in public. Wrong, I know, but everyone makes mistakes. She rang me up and really went to town about the incident a couple of days later. About a week later I had the second champagne dream.

I have often tried to let my friend know of my spiritual feelings towards my close friends, namely forgiveness and unconditional love. For a while she didn't let the incident drop, but rang later, very drunk, to tell me that she loved me and to ask if our friendship was intact.

Before the champagne dreams I truly believed in keeping friendships, even at the cost of my own beliefs. I allowed my friends to dictate to me, thinking they knew better than me about almost everything.

After the second champagne dream I started to assert myself, not in an aggressive way, but with sincerity, empathy and unconditional love. I had no idea how easily influenced I had been, how little I had trusted my own process. Looking back on my decisions with my friends I feel fantastic, knowing I have the power to make my life something wonderful instead of carrying other people's 'baggage' around with me. If I have a conflict with someone, I try to find out what the real problem is.

I learned to let people 'go', to turn the other cheek and wave goodbye, wishing them love and peace and maybe hoping they would learn to love me for who I am. I no longer bury my head in the sand. Now I confront situations head-on, calmly and assuredly, knowing what I want in my life: love, respect, loyalty and a lot of fun!

Kate acquired access to further inner strength through a third dream, one in which she got more in touch with her male side, quite literally!

In this dream an actress, Tina, came into the bathroom and embraced me. She had a penis. I could feel it up against me: it was weird. Then I discovered I had a penis too and woke thinking 'How strange, I'm an androgynous creature, and so is Tina'. In the dream hallway, I remember looking at a huge portrait with fire all around the gilt-edge frame. I asked Tina how the effect was achieved and she explained that it was done by setting chux wipers on fire all around the frame.

I have been assisted in my dream interpretations by a psychologist/hypnotherapist with whom I've been working for a year. I learned from this dream to contact my own powers to stand up for myself, to no longer play on the female side of my nature by being a receptacle in my relationships, whether those friendships be with men or women. I can now be penetrating rather than a receptacle, and no longer need to be 'used' in relationships. I don't need a man and I am starting to balance my Yin and Yang.

The dream also showed me that my relationship with my lover needed cleansing, as depicted by the cleansing flames around the picture of relationship. I realised I wanted more from a relationship than what Nigel could offer me. I wanted a relationship to be as beautiful and perfect as I could make it: 'gilt-edged'.

Physically I had put on heaps of weight since my miscarriage two and a half years ago, and it just seemed to drop off after these dreams. At first this was boosted by a conscious decision to attend Weight Watchers, but now I eat well, still drink the occasional wine and am so active and full of energy that I'm an entirely new person. As Louise Hayes says, 'When you learn to love yourself, miracles happen', or something to that effect!

The last two months of my life have been extraordinary! My life has moved at such a pace, socially and work-wise. I have achieved and accomplished so much in this time and had a lot of fun doing so.

Recently I had two occasions to assert myself — strange circumstances, strange tests — but I did so. I trusted my process of harmony and brought these situations around from potential aggression to harmony and respect. I now feel I have the tools to lead my life on the path I have chosen, working out relationships and going with the energies that make me feel good. I guess the anger I came to the psychologist with in May 1994 has come into balance in some way. Sometimes I still feel angry, but not in the same way as before. I try to find out where it's coming from and work through it, rather than losing my head.

I feel so much more at peace with myself. I try to make peace and forgive all aggressors and I am finding that loving, gracious people are now entering my life instead.

## Jane's Interpretation

Each dream has a similar beginning but concerns a different friend and ends differently. Each relationship, like the champagne offering, is handled in a different way. Since Kate felt comfortable about the ending of each dream, we can assume that her dream choices were appropriate for each relationship. Had she felt unsettled about drinking the first bottle of champagne, for example, or mean for not accepting the champagne gifts in the second dream, her dream handling of each friend would be questioned. A common 'dream couplet' is to have two dreams which start in the same way and have opposite conclusions, but the dreamer feels good about one scenario and uncomfortable about the other. In these cases the dreamer has effectively role-played a difficult situation and decided which felt 'right' for carrying through in waking life. Kate, however, felt pleased with each outcome, so I would interpret this as meaning that each friendship needed to be handled individually.

I would have asked Kate to consider the differences between these two relationships until she could see the benefits in 'letting bygones be bygones' with one, while deciding not to accept the offerings of the other friend no matter how attractively packaged they might appear. The second dream shows Kate's decision to use her own resources, or to express herself in her own way (her own wine), rather than to go along with the friend's style or to be bought by her. Kate had, in fact, looked at her dreams from this angle, and saw the need to check that all her relationships were mutually rewarding.

# Ocean Dip

## Caroline – Warning 1986

I was in a dark room with what appeared to be a hospital bed. Then I felt as if I was not in a hospital but a morgue, and the beds were the tables that are used in morgues for postmortems. I also felt that maybe there were bodies on them. I was by a door and suddenly there was a great sucking sensation dragging me out through the door. All was still dark but I felt as if I was surrounded by awful things and that what was trying to drag me through the door was incredibly evil.

I was not frightened but I was determined that the evil thing was not going to get me through the door. So I hung on to the door jamb and shouted 'No!'. I woke my husband up by grabbing him (as I hung on to the door jamb) and I was actually shouting 'No!' out loud.

I was a solo parent and this dream occurred just before I married my husband. My children were sixteen and eighteen years old. My ex-husband had made life difficult for the previous few years and life was pretty tense around that time.

The intensity and the incredible feeling of evil in the dream was as if someone was trying to get into my mind. I discovered that my eighteen year old son had been dabbling in the occult and I felt that somehow this dream was connected with him and his activities. Although I knew some symbolic meaning was there, I was also aware of a clear warning that I had to act somehow, somewhere.

Shortly after the dream my son turned to spiritualism and I became interested as well. Between 1986 and 1993 I slowly realised that I had to go in a direction which seemed to unfold as if I was being shown a slow motion film, as I discovered myself and my capabilities.

Although my health has deteriorated in some areas, my mind and self-esteem have improved. I have made the correct decision because of the peace that is coming into my life.

## Jane's Interpretation

This kind of dream can indicate the dreamer's fear of death and beyond, but it is more likely to be symbolic of the dreamer's vulnerability to waking life events. Some might interpret this dream as a direct experience of 'evil spirits', but I feel it is more beneficial to examine the dream's symbolism.

The hospital suggests the potential for cure or healing, but the setting rapidly becomes a morgue and the focus is on 'postmortem'. Was Caroline analysing (carrying out a postmortem) on something that had 'died' in her life? The evil, sucking sensation started after noticing the postmortems, so it could be that Caroline was suddenly becoming aware, in going back and analysing her life, that she was being 'sucked' away, no longer in full control of her own life. The hospital setting still shows the potential for healing once Caroline stands up to her discovery, as she does do in the dream, 'hanging on' and screaming 'No!' in defiance.

In interpreting Caroline's dream I would have asked her what she felt had died in her life and in which ways she felt she was losing control. I would then suggest she 'hang on' to the feeling of power and defiance she contacted in the dream to give her the strength to make her 'comeback' in waking life.

The fact that Caroline's son was involved in the occult at the time would have added to her feelings of vulnerability. Being stressed, she would have been susceptible to mind-control by others, living or dead, and her gut reaction to the dream was a good emergency reaction. She strengthened herself against her son's occult interests and joined him when he turned his focus towards a more healing, spiritual path.

As the survey dreamers progressed through their dream-inspired life changes, growing personally through their learning, discovering new abilities and often putting new attitudes and lifestyles into practise, their personal relationships often came under pressure.

Anne, Rowyn and Moni, for example, found they had to move on, to walk a different path:

*Looking back I feel wonderful about what happened. I regret that Andrew couldn't handle the changes and that we couldn't have worked things through together. I became more assertive and wanted, and got, my needs met, which was difficult for him to accept.*

ANNE

*I feel positive within myself and confident I have chosen the right path spiritually but I must confess that at times I feel as if I am leaving others behind. It's like you possess this inner knowing of how events will change or affect others but they don't 'feel' the same sensation. Sometimes it's a lonely feeling. They can't, or won't, comprehend your experiences, dreams or situation, and most of the time if you voice a dream or a feeling, they reply in ridicule and suspicion.*

ROWYN

*In my heart I love them, since I can see only the backgrounds they grew up in and the knots in which they have unwittingly tangled themselves; but loving them is one thing and deciding not to accept the hurt they offer in return is quite another.*

MONI

Others, such as Akira, Francoise and Mary needed time alone to develop and realise their new potential as individuals before relating with their partners in improved ways:

*I travelled and had never felt quite so free. It was the first time in my life since I was a teenager that I had not been in a relationship. There was just me and I realised that life was exciting and that I could do whatever I liked!...I am much more in control. Back with Simon I am now much stronger and know that I am fine, on my own or in partnership.*

AKIRA

Francoise moved away from the family after her dream, and from that perspective reconsidered her relationship with her partner:

*I realised that I still loved this man, but not in the way that it was. Now I have this new strength and foundation, we are re-evaluating our relationship at a more fulfilling level.*

Mary, who had called an end to her relationship just prior to her dream, discovered:

*Eventually, after some years apart and no contact, I met the man again. We had both changed so much, gained in maturity, self-esteem and confidence. We married; now we are very happy.*

Willow and Kate discovered that the changes in their lives resulted in better relationships all, round:

*My attitudes to everything and everyone have been altered for the good and it has made all of my personal relationships so much more satisfying.*

WILLOW

*I feel so much more at peace with myself. I try to make peace and forgive all aggressors and I am finding that loving, gracious people are now entering my life now instead.*

KATE

Perhaps 'life-changing' is too mild a description for some, who felt that their dreams inspired changes which were personally transformational.

*I may still be that person, but only in looks and body structure. On the inside, my thinking and perceptions have changed in a way that is much better than ever before.*

JULIE

*I am now a totally different person. No-one can believe the changes in me. I look younger physically. I used to be so thin, just strained, drained all the time. I've gone back to being a kid again.*

SARRAS

# River 23

## Francoise – The Dolphin 1994

Out of the blue I started travelling. It was like I was travelling in time or through the universe and I found myself travelling through space towards Planet Earth. There it was in front of me. I sailed in, went towards it, and it got bigger and bigger until finally there I was and there was the ocean: beautiful colours, brilliant, indescribable, natural, clear watercolours.

As I got closer there was a big, beautiful wooden sail boat, all made of wood. It seemed to me that it was probably one hundred feet long with beautiful white sails all filled with wind, a hundred sails. It must have been an old boat. It was an eternal boat: that's what it seemed like to me. I kept coming down until I landed on the deck at the top end of the boat. I stood there on the bridge, looking out over the ocean, when a dolphin came out of the water: straight up and out of the water.

As the dolphin came up, its nose and its whole body moved up, right from the tip of my toes all the way up my entire body. It caressed me right up to the top of my head and then continued to leap into the air, such a huge, sensitive, strong, joyous creature. Then it came back down again and disappeared into the water. Throughout all this it made a sound, a deep, knowing, giggling, healing sound, and there was a feeling that accompanied the whole thing, that I'm still feeling now. It's as if I've been touched by some kind of energy that's still here with me.

I turned around and there was a man at the huge, wooden wheel of the boat, sitting in a chair. He had dark brown hair and brown eyes and, although he appeared to be middle-aged, he looked eternal, too. He turned, looked at me and smiled, and I smiled back at him. It was a knowing. The feeling the dolphin had given me was of uplifting happiness, joy and a feeling of aliveness and wholeness.

> I went to bed that night needing an answer. I was totally stressed out, my relationship was falling apart, my personal life was crumbling and everything was disintegrating. I was feeling pressured, bursting at the seams and needing help. I decided that I had to get my life in order and that was that. I called for divine guidance. I was driven subconsciously, somehow knowing my being had to ask.
>
> The dream bathed me in this electric, alive, soothing energy, so much so that I knew that this was my answer. It was so precious to me, it was almost like a sacred passage or initiation. I know beyond a doubt that the life force, or the universal energy of life, or of spirit, whatever you want to call it, is as real as I am holding this telephone. It is there, it's everything. The dream was a divine gift, a beautiful gift of the higher universal energies that are there for the asking. All we have to do is ask.

The dream took immediate effect on Francoise's decision-making.

I decided, OK, I had to step into the unknown, so I moved out on my own. My partner has two children and I have one, all in their mid-teens. I left the kids behind, thinking my son could just go back and forth as he wished. That was the beginning of my disintegration and reintegration.

The very next day I was in the shop going totally gaga over the feeling of what had happened. A lady came in wearing a dolphin T-shirt. I said 'Oh, wow, you're wearing a dolphin T-shirt! I've just had the most amazing dream,' and I told her about it. We started talking and she had just left her man. She bought something from me and when I delivered it to her a week later she gave me a book called *Living in Joy* by Sanaya Roman. I thought, 'What am I going to do with this? Joy? What's that? I know that I don't have any.' I still have the book and it's taken me until now to be able to open it up and say, 'Yes, this is where I'm heading'.

Francoise's process of disintegration and reintegration took place in a very short time: some ten months. Quite simply:

I feel like I've fulfilled one lifetime and I've lightened up and am living another life with much more joy.

So, how did she do it?

I believe that dreams are the Higher Self, or the unconscious, or that energy we all have. 'The Dolphin' was a positive knock on the head, a 'hey woman, wake up' call. I felt like that was the only real thing that was whole and pure in my life at the time. That was what helped me through. I had turned fifty and hit the mid-life crisis. The time was right. It was either 'get your act together or die: become middle-aged and decrepit and disappear to wait for death to come along'. It was like a passage into spirit and it took a lot of trust in myself as well as courage, but I had to do it. It was like my very own personal initiation into freedom and a whole new way of being.

Francoise started by taking hold of her life:

Over a period of ten months I stopped smoking cigarettes, I stopped smoking marijuana, I stopped drinking coffee and eating sugar and I ended up in a black hole because of it. No-one to lean on: no crutches. That was horrible, painful and awful but I knew I had to do this. I did a lot of uncontrollable crying, drank litres of water and did yoga faithfully every day. Moment by moment, day by day, week by week, month by month, I got through. Eventually, slowly, my energy started to change and fill up with a higher vibration source of energy.

As I disintegrated, insights came which helped me deal with the emotional pain I was going through. I think I'm on the other side now because of the contentment, the peace, even joy that's soothing its way into my being.

I had thrown my partner away, like throwing the baby out with the bath water, but I had to kill the relationship totally and not the person. That was painful for him and painful for me. I realised that I still loved this man, but not in the way that I had. Now I have this new strength and foundation, we are re-evaluating our relationship at a more fulfilling level.

He had gone through his thing, his own initiation, a couple of years earlier and he was waiting for me to either shape up or ship out (like the dream?). He sees the changes in me and he loves them. My sensitive son was very supportive. I told him this was something that I had to go through. I think some kids today are much more aware and not as caught up in the emotional stuff I've had to come through.

Although 'The Dolphin' dream caused Francoise to make spectacular changes in her life, she also relished the guidance in a profound dream she had experienced two years earlier:

'The River of Women' is as clear as I am sitting here. We'd gone to a marriage counsellor to try to sort our life out. Our sexual lives were all over the place, naturally when all this stuff happens. We were getting nowhere: I had my side and he had his side. We knew we wanted to hang in there with the relationship but it just wasn't happening for us. I was pretty isolated and it had been my idea to get some type of counselling. Obviously neither of us was as evolved as we are now, or capable of understanding things as we now can. I knew that there were male and female games going on between us and I was trying to identify whose were whose, when I had the dream.

## The River of Women 1992

I was living at the very top of this green, lush mountain, up in the clouds in the blue sky. There was a big wooden shelter which was also a temple at the very top. There was a river going all the way down the mountain, through the valley. Sea level would have been ten miles down, so the river travelled a long, long distance! Normal rivers have rocks which appear to just sit there as the water goes through, over and between them. The further down you go the rocks become smaller, while big boulders and big rocks occur higher up. In this dream, there were no rocks: instead, they were all beautiful, eternal women! There were older women, younger women, ancient women holding newborn female babies and children. They were all sitting and standing in place of the rocks and boulders, relaxed and totally composed, real, alive and totally integrated with nature. They went all the way down to the bottom as far as the eye could see! I was up there wandering around feeling this woman energy: this eternal woman thing.

I took the dream to mean that whatever was happening for me, whatever it was I was trying to express, or feel, or touch and be part of, was being given to me in the dream. I think I was soaking up my feminine side in the dream.

This dream helped Francoise to make progress in the earlier counselling sessions and probably contributed towards the later explosion of changes initiated by 'The Dolphin Dream'. Francoise delights over the changes in her life:

As I get older, I feel like I am getting younger and younger — I feel like I'm a little kid again. I would recommend anyone to follow their intuition and listen to the messages. This is your divine life-force energy talking to you.

### Jane's Interpretation

Such dreams need no further interpretation. They brought Francoise the light she needed to transform her life — and they worked.

# Ocean Dip

## Willow – Precious Jewel 1991

A precious jewel had been stolen from some people like Incas. It was sacred to them. I'm not sure if I had stolen the jewel or not, but I decided to take it back.

The jewel was hidden in the ceiling of a house. When taking it back to its rightful owners, I came across Shirley MacLaine. She was a bad person in the dream, and a fight took place between her and a man. She was wearing a mask which the man took off to reveal her identity, only to find another mask underneath which looked exactly the same. This was her real face.

My marriage had broken up in 1987, four years before this dream. Since then I had been on a search for my own identity, which I felt I had lost during my unhappy marriage.

Most prominent in the dream to me was the mask being removed to reveal another mask that was exactly the same, then the realisation that this was the real face. My physical appearance was always very important to me from my teenage years. I was a model for a short time and I spent a lot of time in front of the mirror, trying out new make-up styles. I used to wear a lot of make-up and would never be seen by anyone without some make-up on.

It was a way of hiding the shy, self-conscious person that I was. This dream showed me that I didn't have to keep hiding behind a mask, that I could let my real self show through. Once the mask was gone it allowed me to explore just who I really was. I felt that during my relationship with my ex-husband, which had started when I was only eighteen, my self-development had come to a complete halt. I am now forty.

I believe the jewel was my own spirituality and gifts such as psychic abilities hidden in the upper recesses of my mind. The fight could have been between the 'anima' (female side) and the 'animus' (male side) struggling for balance in my personality. I had to realise that I am the special person that I always wanted to be.

Willow's understanding of her dreams was an art which she developed over the years, so her final interpretation was perhaps not fully in her consciousness when she originally contemplated the dream. However, she understood it sufficiently to take action and she took her cue from Shirley MacLaine.

The dream made me realise that it is OK to just be me. I don't have to wear masks to be liked or accepted. A matter of weeks after this dream I came across one of Shirley MacLaine books 'by accident' in the library when I was looking for some astrology books. This book led me to her other books and I eventually read them all. Unknown to me at this time, the film version of one of her books, *Out on a Limb*, was being shown on TV.

This whole series of events, which began as a result of this dream, led to a path which I am still following. It has enriched my life and helped me to work through my personal growth, as well as increasing my interest in dreams, which have been a part of my development. I can really help myself and others now. Physically, I used to experience severe back pain and this is now non-existent.

My attitudes to everything and everyone have been altered for the good and it has made all of my personal relationships so much more satisfying. My life has been changed completely. I could never go back to the way I was before.

## Jane's Interpretation

Presumably the Incas represented an ancient sacred wisdom in Willow's mind. Precious jewels in dreams usually symbolise the dreamer's unique and precious self, talents, gifts...a recognition of true inner wealth and value. Willow's sacred connection with life had been stolen. She says, quite wisely in her dream, 'I'm not sure if I had stolen the jewel or not'. We are usually the perpetrators of our own demise. Recognising that you have denied access to a part of yourself, or permitted events and others to rob you of expressing your inner qualities, is the first step to returning to full self-power. Since the jewel was hidden in the ceiling of a house, I would say it represented either an intellectual or spiritual gift (the higher levels of our dream buildings generally being the higher levels of our mind or being).

Shirley MacLaine must have had some personal significance to Willow, or perhaps she appeared in the dream as an actor, being a person who wears masks and plays roles for a living. (That is, until she takes off her masks and writes books to express her personal experiences, beliefs and philosophies.) The fight between Willow's male (Yang) and female (Yin) sides illustrates her struggle, at the time of the dream, between her need for self-expression (Yin and currently masked) and her need to relate to the world at large (Yang). The 'bad' aspect of her Yin is the denial of her true self and the wearing of masks to fit society's (actually her own) expectations of how she should be in the world. The synchronicity of coming across Shirley MacLaine's books shortly after the dream enabled Willow to witness the actor's personal Yin/Yang struggle and subsequent unmasking.

# On Seeking Answers

'Sweet dreams,' we whisper, slipping into the night and joining the greatest magical mystery tour of them all. Many practised dreamers prefer to let go and trust that their dream state will take them to where they need to be, revealing what is important for them to know at that moment. While most of the life-changing steps taken by the dreamers in this book resulted from such 'surprise' dreams, several people did set out to secure an answer to a specific question: and got one.

## River 24

## Beth – Creatures of Habit 1994

I was under a high-set house with my ever present Dream Friend, and we were standing on a dirt floor. All over the floor were little mice and guinea pigs lying on their sides, dead. I was horrified. What had happened to them? Then my cat appeared with a fluffy white guinea-pig in her mouth. 'Put that down,' I ordered her. She laid it down gently on the dirt. I rushed over and examined it

> carefully. It was not injured at all but it was dying. I was about to give it mouth-to-mouth resuscitation and heart massage when my Dream Friend said (I love this friend!) 'Let it die, let it go'.
>
> I still had my hand on the guinea pig. Its coat was soft and silky. I stroked it gently then withdrew my hand, knowing that I could in fact revive it, but I must let it go. I felt OK about making that decision.

I was a cigarette addict for twenty years. I was always giving up, often managed to cut down, and even managed on one or two a day for a while until the stress hit and I would be off again. I spent a fortune on trying to give up smoking, from hypnosis, to subliminal tapes, to acupuncture. You name it, I tried it. In recent years I became a closet smoker. I hated it but couldn't cut it out of my life completely. It didn't make sense: I was a ballet teacher, a vegetarian, a very healthy diet/body-conscious person with a deep, dark secret that I was ashamed of. (OK, life is humorous, eh?) Also it gave me allergic rhinitis.

In 1994 a friend who had done a clinical hypnotherapy course offered to give me hypnotherapy for giving up smoking. Instead of doing it in four days, I suggested we did it over four weeks because it takes at least twenty-one days to change a habit (it also gave me longer to smoke!). We set a 'Cease Smoking' date. Right on course the big day arrived. I knew I wasn't going to be able to do it. I could feel panic arising, along with the well-known sense of failure. I wanted to rush out and buy a packet of cigarettes and smoke like crazy — but a small voice said 'Wait, Beth, ask for help in your dreams tonight'.

So that night, before falling asleep, I beseeched my subconscious to help me be rid of the addiction forever. I knew my conscious mind had a good attitude, but the subconscious was always the saboteur of my best plans.

The result was *powerful*. My smoking habit completely died that night: no withdrawal, no weight gain, no mourning, no bad moods, and just from one dream. Giving up smoking was a really big life-changing thing for me. My family are absolutely astonished, and I am even more astonished. I know now that I will never smoke again. Is this the secret to curing all addictions — drugs, alcohol etc? Funny thing is, dreaming doesn't cost a cent.

So, how did Beth's dream lead to such a powerful change? She sat down in the morning with her dream, knowing it contained the perspective she needed. Beth took the main dream symbols and wrote a list of her own personal associations, feelings and insights alongside each symbol until the plot fell into place. Her dream detective work is exquisite, humorous, yet potently serious in its proven ability to change her smoking habits for good. Over to Beth:

This is truly beautiful: 'Creatures of Habit', of course!

| | |
|---|---|
| Guinea pigs: | happy to be held, need to be fed lots, smelly, die easily. |
| Mice: | cute, courageous, smelly, definitely don't like them in the house. |
| My cat: | a killer, stealthy, will hunt the creatures of habit down. |
| Mouth-to-mouth resuscitation: | the act of smoking. |

Ah yes, the smelly habit that I don't want in my house any more, which needs to die in the subconscious mind. Perhaps I used smoking to 'pet' myself, to stroke and soothe myself. Why I have failed to give up in the past is because I always revive the habit, 'resuscitate' it by allowing myself to have just one cigarette. I must let it die.

Understanding our dreams is one thing, taking action on them is another. Beth used a simple technique to reinforce the message of the dream, to help move it from the subconscious into the hard print of her conscious awareness:

I knew that I must symbolically bury all these little creatures of habit and accept the finality of their death in order to succeed in giving up smoking. I drew five little graves in my Dream Journal and wrote 'Rest in Peace' on the headstones, drew a smoking cigarette on each headstone, and then placed flowers on the graves. I then drew a picture of myself smiling with my cat standing beside me. In a speech bubble above the cat I wrote 'I will help her stalk this habit'.

On reflection Beth realised why the dream had such a positive effect and why it worked over and above other methods she had tried.

We can say affirmations until we are blue in the face but we must simply be brainwashing the conscious mind. My dream had impact because my subconscious informed me of the emotional adjustment needed to achieve my conscious objective. All the conscious mind had to do was say 'Yes, I'll do it'. The act of drawing the picture was confirmation for the subconscious that I had got the message and wished to follow it through.

My result? Success! Naturally my health improved immediately. I was prone to headaches and haven't had a headache since. All changes have been positive. When I think about it I am almost in a state of shock over how easy it was!

## Jane's Interpretation

What more could I possibly say? Beth's analysis of her dream is a perfect example of how to approach a dream full of personal symbolism. Her interpretation was made easier by the fact that she had fallen asleep with the intention of getting to the basics of her smoking addiction. She knew the subject matter and had a couple of good clues such as 'Let it die, let it go' (the smoking habit) and the 'mouth-to-mouth resuscitation', reminiscent of the resuscitating, uplifting effect of a mouth-to-mouth relationship with a cigarette, presumably!

# River 25

## Julie – Zenith 1991

I seemed to be looking at a little girl aged about twelve years old. She was dressed so prettily in all of her splendour in a cream-coloured lace dress and a lovely wide-brimmed hat. It was 'me' and I looked so lovely in the dream, leaning on a table or bench.

Right next to me was a very beautiful and slender lady. She was also finely dressed. Who she was I have no idea, although she could have been my mother. She was holding up an open book to show me that it was mine. I seemed to be an observer in the dream, as I was watching them both. The young girl had her back to me, but I knew she was me, too.

In the front section of the book was an inscription: 'This book belongs to Zenith', and 'Zenith' was me, I thought.

My life was a disaster!! That's what I thought at the time, anyway. My health wasn't too good and I was still getting over the death of my son. I cried a lot and felt lethargic and tired all the time, drained, as though I was a zombie. I was constantly feeling anxiety. So much was triggered off inside me.

I'd put myself in a situation which I'd never wished to happen. I'd put my marriage into jeopardy and my life into turmoil, and, to justify my own behaviour and feelings, I'd put judgements on so many people.

I'd written a letter. I regretted writing it at the time, and why I ever posted it was anybody's guess. I was a very angry person, angry at myself and at others, so all of this came out in my letter.

Now, this letter never reached the person intended, but went to someone else, an uncle, whom I wrote so badly about in the letter. I'd written a number of letters at that time and somehow it got mixed up.

The trouble began when Julie discovered the letter hadn't been received by the person to whom it was intended, but at this stage she had no idea who, out of all the people she had mailed letters to that day, was the recipient of the angry mail.

The guilt began then, because I knew that I had sent it off to someone — but who?! I became paranoid whenever I wrote any letters and would have to check up to see whether the right people had received them. The guilt led to me not wanting to face people in case they saw the real me. I was a mess. I felt my family wouldn't love me any more. Memories from my past began to emerge, although I didn't understand why at the time.

The anxiety was tremendous. I thought of running away: all sorts of things. It would have been one of the most frightening experiences in my entire life, and I'd caused the whole situation, all by myself.

Each night I would pray for answers to reveal who had received the letter. On one of those nights, this dream finally came to me.

I can still see the 'Zenith' dream today, because it had made such a big impact on my life. Because I'd been praying for an answer, the dream stuck in my mind more than the others and it seemed important to me to know the dream's meaning. I'm not too sure how many days it was before I worked out what the dream had meant to me. I know it was only a short time, but it was a dream that didn't leave me. I persisted, like an obsession, until the meaning came and I found out how important it was to me. I was so shocked by my findings.

The word 'Zenith' had stumped me. I decided to look up the dictionary to see if it was there. Sure enough, it was and I took it as 'the highest point in the universe'. OK. Now that was established I thought 'What is the highest point in the universe to me? God. God is the highest point in the universe. Yes!!'

'But what's God got to do with this dream?', I thought. Somehow it hit me. 'This book belongs to 'Zenith' must mean 'This book belongs to God'. I raced to get my Bible, opened it up to the front of the book and there was a card from my uncle, right in the front page. I nearly died when I saw the card. I had forgotten I'd put it there. I knew then who I had posted the letter to by mistake.

Realising what 'Zenith' had meant to me set the ball rolling to interpret the dream. I wondered what the age or number twelve had to do with the dream. I turned to page twelve in the Bible and read the contents: it was all about judgement. I knew it was the right answer for me. Just after I had worked all this out, I had confirmation that it was my uncle who had received the letter. Not only had the 'Zenith' dream been of great importance to me, but also my prayers had been answered.

I'd probably been getting close to the answer because I'd had a dream the week before that I was way up in the universe (zenith) looking down onto a map. The dream zoomed in, as if through a camera, onto this map and then a star shape landed on the map, sort of like 'x marks the spot'.

The changes to my life started within a week or so after interpreting my dream. Firstly, I didn't want to be that person any more. I wanted to change. I didn't like the person that I was. I knew then that my whole way of living had to change, otherwise I would stay the same.

I wrote letters off to various people who were mentioned in 'the letter' that I'd written a couple of months before the dream. I apologised to them for what I had said, even though they had no idea. I felt it was something that I had to do at the time. I had some good responses from some people, but others didn't answer. It was very difficult writing and sending off those letters.

I'd already been going to a counsellor for a short time for something else. Someone had put me onto a Women's Group where I also went to gain self-esteem, confidence and so on. I began to learn more about who I was and what I was about. I kept going to various groups, learning more about myself. I wanted to keep on learning.

I feel now that the whole experience was meant to happen. It taught me a good lesson about judgement of other people and really made me look at myself. I now know the hurt and pain I caused to so many people, including myself, and that's a big lesson for one to learn.

I may still be that person, but only in looks and body structure. On the inside, my thinking and perceptions have changed in a way that is much better than ever before.

In a dream which took place about three weeks after 'Zenith', I was saying goodbye to a lot of young people and I remember saying, in the dream or as I was waking up: 'I wish you all, through life, an abundance of peace, love and happiness.'

Out with the old, on with the new.

## Jane's Interpretation

To interpret this dream I would have started by asking Julie what 'Zenith' meant to her. If she was completely mystified I probably would have suggested 'highest point', and therefore perhaps 'higher self'. The term 'higher self' has a wide spectrum of meanings today, but I use it to denote an ideally pure viewpoint, a 'highest perspective' such as we might gain by standing back and taking an entirely objective, non-judgemental, loving look at ourselves and our situation. Julie's dream reinforces this interpretation because it was experienced as an objective onlooker.

I would have interpreted the book as representing a source of knowledge. In her dream, Julie felt this book belonged to her, so I would have concluded that everything Julie needed to know could be accessed through her higher self. Subconsciously, of course, Julie knew exactly who she had posted the letter to. All she needed to do was let her subconscious mind take over and reveal the answer: which she, and it, did!

# Ocean Dip
~
# Caz – To Remain or Not to Remain Married? That is the Question 1993

> I asked Marissa whether or not to go to London to reunite with Christopher. The communication I received from her was 'don't go!'

I had married Christopher in the UK in August 1990 but by May 1991 I felt our relationship was floundering. By the following August we began a three month trial separation and, six months later, I left the UK to spend two months travelling in Egypt and Thailand en route to Australia. Back home, I spent several months in a familiar environment with my sister and her family before meeting Christopher again at the end of 1992 to holiday together in Thailand. We are both born travellers. By February 1993 initial decisions were being made to reunite with him and move back to England. By May, the time of my dream, my body symptoms as well as the dream were indicating to the contrary.

Marissa is a spiritual healer and a person whom I love unconditionally. Earlier that evening, before the dream, I went to an evening workshop on personal growth with Marissa as facilitator, after having spent a weekend in confusion over Christopher, and feeling a pain inside my lower left back. I desperately wanted Marissa to answer my question, but I was not able to present it that evening, let alone get an answer. To add to this, I discovered Marissa was now off to the UK for a month or so. I feel she would have sensed my need for an answer to my urgent question and given it to me in my dream.

Before sleep that night I prepared myself to recall with clarity my dreams, falling asleep to the affirmation 'Harmony and peace, love and joy surround me and dwell in me'. I asked Marissa whether or not I should go to London to reunite with Christopher. The communication I received from her was 'don't go!'

On the morning following the dream, before I awoke and had a chance to record details on paper, Christopher rang and I expressed my change of plans. My unconditional love and trust in Marissa had led me to perceive her dream answer as a direct translation. I still carried through with my garage sale the next weekend, because it was a much needed 'letting go' of many things in my past anyway.

For a short while after this, I probably found my ego or consciousness interpreting my dreams in an overriding fashion, seeking confirmation or approval that I had made the right decision. Looking back, had I known how to perceive my bodily symptoms, even on the eve of my wedding, the answer and actions should have been 'No. Stop' way back then.

I have no regrets. The decision snowballed into an intense year of working on myself and a commitment to continue to do so. In December 1994 I spent a month travelling on holiday in Australia with Christopher and remain convinced and relieved that we did not reunite. I felt myself floundering and losing my identity even within a month. I would rather be dead to obtain freedom, than suffocate in the relationship. No matter how strong my self-esteem, it would just get chipped away and erode. It wouldn't be strong enough to survive!

Caz is highly aware of the way in which the body reflects the mind, and now capably uses this as a diagnostic barometer of her subconscious feelings.

Before the dream I had pain inside my lower left back due to feeling unsupported in all aspects of the relationship, especially Christopher's lack of commitment to personal awareness which would have benefited the relationship. Since the age of thirteen, I have suffered from idiopathic oedema. Curiously, during the two months spent travelling in extreme heat in Egypt and Thailand, I suffered no oedema. I guess this was because I was not under any stress of expectations, particularly from men. Within a few months of returning to Australia, I was caught up emotionally in a past relationship and the oedema flared and has not really subsided since.

Interestingly, within two days of being in Christopher's company during our recent shared holiday, my body reacted strongly. My legs became tree trunks, twice as thick as their normal size. The feeling was that I was carrying him around as part of me and that I had to pull all the weight for the pair of us. My brain was working for the two of us. I am usually reluctant to use clinical medicines but weakened under the circumstances of some intensive travelling within that month. Further, upon Christopher's immediate departure, at the airport, I could feel a huge weight lift from me. Within one week, the extent of the fluid retention in my feet had reduced substantially.

Fascinating stuff, how inappropriately-dealt-with emotions reveal themselves in bodily symptoms!

## Jane's Interpretation

There are no details to interpret! The rule of thumb for assessing advice received in a dream is simple: if it feels right when weighed up in the cool light of day, follow it.

Francoise's cry for help was more generally phrased:

*I decided that I had to get my life in order and that was that. I called for divine guidance. I was driven subconsciously, somehow knowing my being had to ask.*

Her dream responded with a power which knocked her off her feet and into a new way of being.

Sarras's plea came, not in a dream, but in her waking life moments after aborting her attempt to commit suicide:

*I was lying on the floor saying 'Please, Jesus, help me'. I'm not a religious person, so I was thinking 'Where did that come from?', but I guess that's the point you get to. It's the only thing you can think of, to ask for help. All of a sudden I remembered the beautiful face from my dream.*

It was her recollection of a vision from her dream that came to her rescue, giving her hope and the inspiration to climb up from rock bottom and into her new life.

Moni did not consciously take a question to bed with her, but she had decided to postpone a decision and sleep on it:

*Since the letter was couched in strong terms and I was mentally and physically exhausted, I decided I should at least sleep well and reconsider it when I was refreshed. The letter could sit to one side for a while.*

Her dream put her into a situation where she was forced to decide whether to drop her letter in the litter bin or to hand it over to the person concerned:

*On waking I knew that since I had made the decision in my dream to hand over the letter, believing the situation to be real and being totally satisfied with my action, that I should follow through and post the letter. I had no doubt at all about this. The dream did not add fuel to my fire; it added concrete below my feet.*

Like Moni, Jayne's dream was a role play of a decision she needed to confirm:

## Ocean Dip

### Jayne – Decision 1992

I was wearing a white wedding dress and walking down a corridor when I saw a man sitting on a seat. I knew him really well in the dream (but not in waking reality). He had his head down and he was crying.

I went and put my arms around him and he said,'You shouldn't go ahead. You really shouldn't be doing this'. I reassured him: 'Look, don't worry, everything will be all right'. As I emerged from the corridor, my daughter came up to me and urged 'Mum, hurry up, because they're all waiting for you to start the ceremony'.

I looked at her and I said 'Priscilla, I don't think I'll be going through with it. I just can't go through with it.' 'You've got to, everyone's waiting for you,' she said. 'No. That's it. I don't want to do it,' I answered. I walked into a room where my boyfriend was and he was all dressed in his tuxedo ready for the wedding. 'Look, I'm sorry,' I said, 'but I can't go through with it.'

He accepted it. He wasn't happy, but then he wasn't happy in himself at the time anyway, so it didn't surprise me.

I was having a relationship with this gentleman, John, who was divorced and living with his three children. We were going to move in and live together and I was really bending backwards to make the relationship work, but it was rocky. I was so undecided as to whether to continue. I had two children of my own and my daughter was hassling me that if he moved in with his children then she was moving out. All three of his kids were really boisterous so it was a very big decision I had to make.

During these months of uncertainty, Jayne had a recurring series of dreams, which ultimately led to her final, life-changing dream, as described above.

In each dream I was getting ready to be married. I would be going shopping, always for different things, but it was basically the same dream. I might be shopping for a veil with my mother, for a headpiece with my sister, or preparing for something for the wedding with my daughter. They were always women on my side of the family. In the middle of shopping I would turn round and say 'Look, I don't think I can go through with this'.

I was married before for nineteen years and that was a disaster. In each dream, as I was picking each wedding object, there was a fear inside me. I guess my fear was that the minute we moved in he'd be a different person altogether.

I had the final dream when I was more or less a hundred per cent certain that it would not work out and that I wouldn't go through with it. I was so definite in the dream, that I thought 'That's it. That's the answer to all my questions.' It had been a hard decision to make but once I'd made it I felt a lot better.

I just cut all the ties completely and straight away. It took me ages to get over him and to get over the fact that there was nothing left there, but in the end I was happier. The wedding dreams were over and John has never entered my dreams since.

Now we work together and that's all. There's nothing left at all of the relationship and I have no regrets. In fact, we are better friends now than we ever were before.

## Jane's Interpretation

Jayne would never have asked me for an interpretation of her dream because it so obviously confirmed her waking life feelings. It was a role-playing dream which helped her to experience calling off the wedding, wake up, assess the dream and her feelings, and gather the courage to follow through with cancelling the relationship plans. The first question I would ask a dreamer who tested me with a similar dream would be 'Are you planning on getting married or affirming a relationship?' If a dreamer with wedding plans consulted me with a dream like this, horrified by the dream because it contradicted her waking life feelings, I would look for symbolic content.

One important symbolic character in Jayne's dream, though, is the man who was sitting crying. As Jayne remarked, 'I knew him really well in the dream (but not in waking reality)'. When we meet a person or an aspect of ourselves in a dream with whom we readily identify, we instantly have this feeling of familiarity and closeness. People often interpret such characters as 'guides' presenting themselves at the dream level, and this may also be the case. Certainly the information or advice they give is usually wise and well worth following. In my own dreams I treat such familiar dream souls with great reverence. If this man was symbolic of Jayne's higher wisdom, then his advice was invaluable. If he was symbolic of her inner male, then he represented her outer life (her Yang qualities such as interest in her career, assertiveness, intellectual self, logic, rational thought), which may well have been areas of her life she perceived as being threatened by her future marriage.

## River 26

## Arthur – Little Dove 1991

> A little dove is very young and immature. I ask 'What shall I do?' and a man said 'Give it some nourishment'. With that the man squeezed the orange he was eating and a couple of drops of orange juice fell to the ground. This little bird drank up the juice and then settled down and started to preen its feathers. I said I would take it home and nourish it.

I'm not sure yet whether this series of dreams and what happened has been life-changing, but it has all been very confusing.

The dreams and related events of the last few years have certainly challenged Arthur's understanding of life, causing him to study, research and think deeply about the nature of dreams.

It all started, as far as I'm concerned, when Alice was looking after this old war veteran called Pete. Now the set-up was, Pete would pay off the house and Alice would take care of him in return, a good arrangement for both of them, when Pete wasn't on the booze.

Now this started when Alice was feeling poorly. Pete had had a few and he gave her this soup he had heated up, but didn't tell Alice that he had put in some of his tranquillisers that would down a horse, let alone someone who weighed just over fifty kilos.

Anyway I received this phone call from Alice that I could not understand and decided to ask one of her friends if she would come with me to Alice's place, as I thought she was sick, so we had better go and check it out.

When we got there both were pretty incomprehensible, but when we finally found out what he had done we called the ambulance and had her taken to the hospital to get pumped out. They kept her under observation in intensive care overnight.

I had been reading about Edgar Cayce and how important dreams were and was wondering what I could do for the situation, so I asked, just before going to sleep, what I could do to help. I received the little dove dream that night.

Arthur's commitment to care for Alice continued for some time, and over the events of the next year or so he gradually became aware of the connection between this woman and some of his earlier dreams.

Prior to my dove dream I had had two others about this lady dressed in white.

In the first, a very nice looking lady appeared to me dressed in a white suit. Her features were quite heart-shaped. When I think back it might have been a nun's habit, because around her head all was white and I could not see her hair.

A few months later, in the second dream, a lady and myself had just stopped and parked the car. Another car was parked behind us with two people sitting inside. When we got out and started walking, two men got out of the car and came towards us and started to menace us. I called out 'Dear Lord, protect us, for they know not what they do'. Next moment they were both writhing on the ground. They then got up and went to their car and drove off at great speed. Some people we knew came up and we told them what had happened but they took some convincing. The lady was dressed in white.

Around ten months after I had the dream of the lady with the heart-shaped face, I attended a Psychic Fair locally and I asked Maryanne if she needed anyone to do hands-on healing. So down I went this Saturday morning, full of good intentions, but there was no room to do any healing and so I gave my friend Len a hand to sell raffle tickets. Then I saw these drawings on the wall and Len told me the lady is a psychic artist. I decided to have one of those drawings done, which I did. When the lady had just about finished I got the shock of my life and I said to her 'I have had a couple of dreams about that lady, the only difference is she was in white and you have drawn her in blue'. I guess it would be pretty hard to draw someone white on white paper.

My final dream, so far, about the lady in white was in May 1992.

In the dream I met my beautiful lady and talked to her. She said that I had promised her that I would get in touch with her mentally, when I first met her in my dreams.

For the next eighteen months things went reasonably well with Pete and Alice and then they sold out and went overseas for a while. Pete stayed overseas, but Alice came back and went up North to work so I didn't see her for nearly twelve months. She related to me the following incident:

She had this small car and decided to go for a trip to Mt Isa on her own. Around Charters Towers, she thinks, she took a wrong turn and finished up out in whoop whoop and nearly out of petrol, when she came across this young helicopter pilot who gave her some petrol and a feed. As it was getting dark she asked if she could stay there for the night and leave early in the morning, which she did.

Back on the main road she saw this couple walking along and stopped to give them a lift. Being a couple she thought she would be safe. The man had tattoos on his arms and looked quite the unsavoury type. After they had been going for a while he asked her to stop the car and they got out. Next minute he knocked the woman out and left her lying on the road and got back into the car and told Alice they were going to Adelaide.

When they had been going for a while he wanted to stop and have a bit by the side of the road. Alice said 'Let's wait 'til we get to the next town and do it properly and stay at a motel'. He agreed to that and the next thing he was asleep, so, very carefully, she turned the car around and headed back to Mt Isa. It is very hard to know which way one is going in that type of country unless you know where the sun should be. The guy woke up and wanted to know where they were and she said 'Go back to sleep, it's not far now. I will wake you up when we get to the town.'

She woke him all right when she pulled up at the Mt Isa police station and a big cop was standing outside the car door. She told the police what had happened. They got the money off him and then she hightailed it back to Cairns as fast as her car would go. She was a very lucky young lady.

I guess one of my dreams was telling me she was well protected. Her guardian angel was looking after her that day. Over the period I had a few little dreams about her, but never thought much about them: she was gone and I might never see her again.

Later I heard a knock on the door and lo and behold it was Alice and I said 'This is a surprise'. Over the next few weeks she called a few times and didn't seem to know why she was there. Then she told me she needed this operation on her nose. She had fallen down some stairs and had broken her nose. The doctors had done cosmetic surgery before and put silicon in and she wanted it removed and needed a few dollars to pay for the operation.

She had told me the day of the operation but never what time it would be. On the day I went out to water the garden about 8.45 am and I could not get her out of my mind. What the hell is going on? A couple of weeks later she came back and paid the money she owed me and I asked 'What time was your operation?' She said 'It was supposed to be at 11.15 but they moved it forward to 9.15'.

Just after this she visited and said 'I won't be back again, wish me luck'. So I wished her good luck, shook her hand, and she was gone. As soon as she had gone out the gate this little voice spoke to me, 'She will be back when she is sick'.

A few weeks after this I decided to visit a friend down south for the weekend. I had been asked months before and decided to make the effort. Driving down I could not get Alice out of my mind, and the only thing I could do was send her love in my mind, which I did. The next day, driving home, the same thing happened, so I kept on sending love to her. What was going on?

About 2 am on the Monday morning I was woken up by a very bedraggled person standing over me saying, 'Can you help me?' What a mess! I got her cleaned up with a shower and gave her something to eat, and while this was going on she was telling me that she had been walking around outside Ipswich trying to get to Sydney. I said, 'You can tell me tomorrow, but now you need some sleep'. This is what she told me the next day:

She had driven her car to Brisbane on the way to Sydney and had no money in her pocket. It was getting late and she met this very kind lady who got her a bed in a backpacker's hostel. The room was divided by a curtain, and the chap behind it, who was having a beer, asked her if she wanted a drink. She told him 'No thank you'. He then asked if she would like to have a read of the Bible he had, and she said she would like that. After she had been reading for a while she thought the bloke was asleep, yet any questions she asked in her head about the things she was reading were answered by the bloke in the next room. All through this adventure she told me she knew what she was doing, but just couldn't seem to help herself.

Next morning she thanked the people and started walking to Ipswich. How far out of town she didn't know, but she got picked up by this Maori fellow who was a minister of some church and he gave her ten dollars to help her along her way. Next, when she was walking along the road with no houses about, this hoon tried to run her over, so she decided to walk through the scrub off the road. She was walking along and she thought someone was following her, so, as she was wearing a white dress and white underclothes, she threw them all away so she would be harder to see and laid down in the grass or what there was of it. After nothing to eat for two days and nothing to drink all that day she was getting pretty near exhausted. She finally came across this house with a towel on the line, draped it around herself and knocked on the door. The lady of the house came to the door and she asked for a glass of water. In all she drank seven glasses of water. The kind lady gave her some clothes and then rang the police and they came and picked her up. When they questioned her it had been them that had been following her in the bush.

After that they took her to the Ipswich toll road booth where the lady in the booth got her a ride to my house.

Arthur had nourished his little dove and taken her home whenever she needed the rest. The connections between the lady in white of his dreams, his little dove, the artist's psychic drawing and the way in which his dreams and daytime feelings intertwined with Alice's adventures have left him questioning the meaning of it all.

## Jane's Interpretation

Doves often represent peace, while birds in general can symbolise the spirit or soul: flight and freedom. Perhaps the dove is a spiritual symbol of peace, and in Arthur's case, spiritual inner peace was fledgling, growing, but young and needing attention and special nourishment. In his dream state Arthur is aware of his spiritual needs and asks how to help himself grow. Unless an orange had a special significance to Arthur, the dream interpretation might focus on the colour orange. In meditation, which Arthur did practice, orange generally symbolises harmony and peace. So the dream already reveals two symbols of peace: the dove and the colour orange. Essentially the dream advises Arthur to take what he has learned (the fruit of his learning?) on a spiritual level about peace and harmony and to let it fuel his own needs. Living in a peaceful, harmonious way encourages further growth. The way to peace and harmony is to let it work in your own life. He had to 'take it home and nourish it', just as he had to take peace and harmony into his own heart and live it.

This is all on an inner level. What happened in Arthur's life, as it so often does, is that the outer world also presented him with an opportunity to apply his learning at the same time. He extended love to Alice, whom he saw as a little dove in need of nourishment, taking her into his home and his heart. By expressing his tenderness and helping someone else in this way, his own inner world was simultaneously enriched and nourished. Peace and harmony grew both in Arthur's inner and outer worlds.

With our eyes open we see that what passes in our outer world of relationships and events is often a metaphor of a parallel development within our inner world, our psyche, our self. In waking life, the world around us mirrors our inner personal development. When we make rapid inner changes, our outer world situation shifts too. This is why it is instructive to look at each dream on an inner level, even if an outer level dream interpretation is extremely obvious. Taking action at the inner level first, even though this may seem too ethereal or remote, often causes the greatest and fastest changes in the simultaneous outer world. Dream interpretation can take you as deep as you wish to go: the choice of action is yours.

Answers, decisions...all you need to know to change your life, or maybe just to smooth it along a little, may be contained in a single moment in a dream.

*The dream was a divine gift, a beautiful gift of the higher universal energies that are there for the asking. All we have to do is ask.*

FRANCOISE

# On Crisis

Of the forty-five dreamers who contributed their life-changing dreams for this book, fourteen had reached a crisis point in their lives and six of these could be described as being in a state of major crisis. A further ten were suffering stress, while twenty-one either reported that nothing out of the ordinary was happening, or that they were feeling mildly stressed. The interplay between crisis, stress and dream content has been discussed throughout this book. A strong relationship between major personal crisis and the experience of intensely spiritually-charged dreams is discussed in the chapter 'On Spirituality, Universal Life Force & God'.

# On Impact

In this dream survey, the life-changing dream years evenly spanned several decades. The most distant dream took place thirty years ago, and three others occurred more than twenty-four years in the past, yet their impact has reverberated throughout time. These dreams remained, for most contributors, as fresh and emotionally charged as they were when they first exploded into the night.

What is it about one particular dream, compared to years and years of dreaming, that really stands out and causes someone to take life-changing action? Specifically I asked 'Why did this dream have so much impact on you? For example, what really stood out in the dream and why did it affect you so much?'

Top of the list for a precise answer was 'clarity' or 'it was so real!' Seven of the forty-five dreamers were confident that these were the most important factors in creating impact.

*It wasn't just another 'dream'. It wasn't hazy...it happened.*
*It was as real as sitting here writing about it.*
CHERYL

*It was so clear and precise, so real.*
*I just 'knew' it was to be acted on.*
SUE

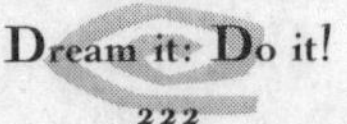

*This dream had so much impact on me because through all our years of infertility I had never experienced a dream which was so clear and positive. In previous dreams involving birth I never reached the point of delivery.*

ANNIE

*I have had vivid dreams in the past, but none more than this. The clarity and 'realness' were incredible. I can remember this dream I had in July 1994 clearer than I can remember a recent trip to Sydney. Although it was not lucid, there was nothing in the dream to indicate it was a dream. There was nothing bizarre. Nothing strange or surreal happened. In short, nothing out of the ordinary at all happened. And that is exactly what really stood out. It was, and I can't say it any clearer, 'too real'.*

ANDY

*What stood out was how clear the dream was. The name of the hospital, the interviewing board, the time given. Somehow there was a knowing that the message was a strong one.*

JAQUIE

Although seven dreamers were quick to answer 'clarity' or 'real' as their high impact factor, I noticed that ten dreamers all referred to strong 'feelings' in their responses. Dreams which hit the 'feeling spot' go deep and have maximum effect, it seems.

*The face: I can still see it and feel the feeling that went with it. I am not a church person, but it was like a religious experience... The feeling of being surrounded by love.*

SARRAS

*The feeling of peace. Peace of mind that I had forgotten existed. Once experienced, it became like a magnet, drawing me towards the direction in which the dream pointed.*

HEATHER

*It left me feeling so shocked that I knew I absolutely had to take action.*

AKIRA

*The intensity. The incredible feeling of evil and the feeling that someone was trying to get into my mind.*

CAROLINE

*The feeling part: the fact that I felt it. I've had many dreams that were significant but this one was so connected to the feeling part that it was eerie.*

HARRY

Realisation was an impact factor for four people. In our dream state we are far more open to insight about our situation or attitudes simply because we tend to repress self-knowledge during our waking lives.

*The impact of the dream was indescribable. The realisation that nothing external was responsible for my situation, that the whole cause and solution rested with me, was comparable to a bolt of lightening.*

MELL

*...the mask being removed to reveal another mask that was exactly the same, and the realisation that this was the real face.*

WILLOW

*I could let myself go downhill even more or I had the power to make changes in my life.*

MICHAELA

*What really stood out in the dream was the island being flooded by sea water and that was the same in my life.*

DEE DEE

Other important factors in creating impact included:

- a sense of reassurance:

*The strongest impact it had was to reassure me that I did have a place in the universe, that I was not alone and that there is something other than the visible, tangible world around us.*

LORNA

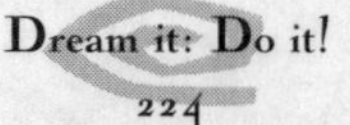

• light infusing the dream:

*The dream had a shiny white light around the edges of it.*
ZOHARA

• a sense of life-purpose:

*I felt that my life did have a purpose.*
*I didn't feel so alone any more.*
ANNE

• and the experience of trying out, or role-playing, apparently for real:

*What stood out in the dream was that I had the courage*
*to tell people to get off my back.*
DEE DEE

# On Taking Action

The time gap between having the dream and making the life-changes proved an interesting question. Fifteen people acted immediately, while five took action within the first week. Six people let a month or so lapse, while another six dreamers waited somewhere between a couple of months and a year. The remaining eight saw a more long-term plan come into play, one quoting seven years from dream to fruition, and most witnessing a delay of at least two years prior to realising the changes.

Some found the question of the time gap between the dream and the subsequent life changes a difficult one to answer, having acted immediately but having only seen the full benefits much later:

*The changes to my life…were almost immediate in a slow process. I took the steps very slowly, integrating my spirituality into my life calmly and slowly.*

ANNE

Others felt the change was passive rather than active:

*It changed me rather than encouraging me to change my life through any external action.*

LORNA

For some the message was so powerful that immediate action was instigated:

*The change began immediately. The dream made me see the whole situation for what it was — in a way which made instantaneous and total sense.*

MELL

While others had already asked a question and were armed to put their dream answer into use the next day:

*Instant. Urgent question received an urgent answer!*

CAZ

While life-changing action was purely the result of one dream for twenty-seven contributors, thirteen people attributed their changes to a series of dreams, usually sparked by, or culminating with, the major one. Only six life-changing dreams were recurring, either in detail or in general theme. Three dreamers specifically counted two dreams as being of equal and combined importance in their decision making.

# On Regrets

When I invited people who felt they had changed their lives as a result of a dream to contribute their experience for this research, I was prepared for some stories of regret. I had made a point in many of my media interviews of asking people to come forward regardless of whether the outcome had turned out to be to their advantage or to their disadvantage. I didn't wish to exclude negative experiences in favour of projecting an entirely positive report.

In fact, of the numerous enquiries and offers I received, not one person had a tale of regret. All agreed that the changes had been worth the risks.

Having read their stories, you may agree that some of their actions led to challenging or stressful circumstances, to say the least, but the perception of each dreamer remained positive. They generally felt embraced by the strength and insight they had gained from the experience.

*If I'd wanted an easy life, I shouldn't have moved, but I couldn't have grown to where I am now if I had stayed where I was. I guess, looking back, a lot of things here just happened so that I could experience the dark side of myself. Up until that point, I'd probably been a goody-two-shoes, which it was easy to be since I've always had guidance. I've always had a guardian angel sitting on my shoulders! My dark side has shown me emotions such as anger, even resentment*

*and other feelings that were alien to my nature until we moved here. I can see that you can't help people in difficult situations unless you've experienced them too. It doesn't matter what it is you're helping people with, words are empty unless you've been through that experience.*
*[Now]...I have a sense of very deep peace and contentment here.*
ZOHARA

Anne, Rowyn and Moni mentioned some regret at losing close relationship with people who had previously been important to them, but each was able to put their loss into a metaphysical context. Each simply had to move on, no longer able to restrict their own development for the sake of others. Otherwise the general consensus is summarised by Akira when she says:

*My only regret is that it took me so long to take many of the actions that followed the dream.*
AKIRA

# On Health & Wellbeing

While some dreamers experienced a downturn in their physical health following their life-changing dream, the majority reported improvement. For some, physical symptoms increased before they returned to health. Harry, for example, felt he put his health in jeopardy for the sake of rebirth.

*If anything my health went down because of my process of thinking through the thing and bringing myself into turmoil. I tend to bring myself right down to bottom and then look at myself in the mirror and say 'What's going on in here?'*

Peter found that both the stress of pursuing his life-changes and the resulting shock to his system took their toll before he regained control and put himself back on the road to health and recovery.

*Searching for my natural parents was a very stressful time but it was something that I had to do...After the dream, and after I discovered my father again, I just went into shock and ended up again at the doctors.*

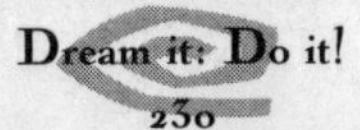

Akira's symptoms continued after her dream while she herself continued the process of working on the insights revealed by the experience.

*I had physical difficulties — exhaustion, loss of weight, anxiety. My eyes became weaker (and I was aware there was stuff in my life I didn't want to see). I experienced these things before, during and after the dream.*

Heather's health followed a similar pattern as she spent time, following her move, on researching the ground revealed by the stones her dreams had turned. Rowyn's physical health has deteriorated during the years she has been learning through her dreams, although her academic performance has excelled.

The majority of dreamers identified stresses or specific bodily symptoms, diseases, aches, pains or accident proneness which were present at the time of their dreams, but which either improved or disappeared as a result of their subsequent life-changes.

*At the time of the dream I had terrible neck pain. Just before this I had flu for two months. In the middle of the two dreams I had a car accident and hit a post (I was blinded by the sun and didn't see a traffic island!). My back and neck are now fine.*

CALLI

*I do know that my health has gradually improved since then. I used to experience severe back pain and this is now non-existent.*

WILLOW

*My physical and emotional health had been low for some time before the dream. My general health had been deteriorating for several years. I had recently had flu followed by pneumonia. I was experiencing frequent severe migraines and minor bouts of asthma... [After the dream] my general health and that of the children improved steadily.*

LORNA

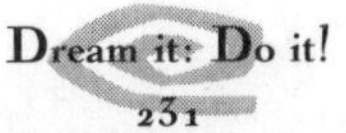

*I was quite sick physically following my first child's birth and back problems ensued...But I am pretty amazingly healthy now and have been for a long time.*

SUSANNAH

Metaphors of physical symptoms reflecting emotional patterns were spotted by Caz, Mell, Grace, Akira and Michaela, amongst others:

*Using kinesiology, the specific parasite was identified and a remedy prescribed to purge it from my body. This was a fine physical metaphor for what I was going through on other levels.*

GRACE

Grace's story reveals the truth of her statement, and her postscript, sent to me in the last week of preparing the manuscript for this book, adds a further dimension to her metaphor. Grace's dream led her to approach her childhood and her relationship with her parents in a new light. In so doing, it seems, the purging has benefited her mother as well as the mother-daughter relationship itself:

*My visit to Melbourne was a big healing time for all my family, most dramatically in the form of my mother having a tumorous piece of colon surgically removed at the same time that I was at the family therapist!*

GRACE

*Before the dream, when things were really bad, I realise now I was unusually accident-prone. I can think of several incidents, in particular, and all of them were injuries to legs, ankles, feet, etc. Having since read a bit of what Louise Hayes has to say about problems related to various parts of the body — well, it makes you wonder!*

MELL

(Louise Hayes, in her book *Heal Your Body*, suggests that legs symbolise carrying us forward in life, feet represent our understanding and ankles our mobility and direction: all pertinent to Mell's experiences.)

Michaela was mentally and emotionally broken down:

*By the time I was twenty-nine years old my body had totally broken down. I needed help but I did not know where to go. This dream was the turning point...I have perfect health now.*

As Akira's comment earlier in this section illustrates, she interpreted her weakening eyes as symptomatic, on a symbolic level, of 'stuff in my life I didn't want to see'.

Caz was considering whether or not to reunite with her husband, following a trial separation:

*Before the dream, I had pain inside my lower left back...I was feeling unsupported in all aspects of the relationship...*

After the dream, during a holiday together with her husband, Christopher, Caz observed:

*Interestingly, within two days of being in Christopher's company during our recent shared holiday, my body reacted strongly. My legs became tree trunks, twice as thick as their normal size. The feeling was that I was carrying him around as part of me...Upon Christopher's immediate departure, at the airport, I could feel a huge weight lift from me. Within one week, the extent of the fluid retention in my feet had reduced substantially. Fascinating stuff, how inappropriately dealt-with emotions reveal themselves in bodily symptoms!*

Lee noticed:

*If I have lapses where I don't attempt anything creative, I have very troubling dreams where I get attacked by a snake, usually biting my right hand. I'm sure it tries to wake me up and get me moving.*

It's pertinent to note that Lee had injured her right index finger, severing some nerves, several years before her life-changing dream, and that she had gone into hospital a few months before her dream to have an operation to restore some use. In dream language, or in body/mind language (which is much the same), the right hand tends to represent how we use our creativity in the world, how we operate in the world at large, while the fingers tend to symbolise the small details of this handling.

Lee's dilemma, addressed by her life-changing dream, concerned her need to move away from using her creative skills in the commercial art world and towards expression in fine art and writing. Perhaps she had lost feeling for the commercial work, symbolised by the severing of the nerves in her waking life. No wonder a dream snake bites her right hand to get her moving when she lapses on her creativity. Interestingly, snakes in dreams often represent the need to face pain to gain healing, so perhaps Lee's work needs to touch on difficult areas to be ultimately satisfying for her.

The 'body/mind' describes the way in which the physical body seems to mirror the mind. Physical symptoms, ailments or disease generally surface in our lives when we have missed a previous 'alert' cue from the mind. Our dreams often address emotional issues which, if left unheeded, frequently solidify into the physical body. If no-one is listening at the dream level, it seems, a higher profile message needs to be relayed! The majority of life-changing dreams presented in this book have triggered the dreamer to identify long-held barriers to growth, or to inspire them to take long overdue moves. If the body/mind is as powerful as observation suggests, it will come as no surprise to discover that changing a life through addressing an issue often results in physical recovery and a return to full health and wellbeing.

# River of Dreams

## The Sequel

This final chapter, your own life-changing dream, is for you to dream, to do and to tell. Swim with tranquillity in your river of dreams, go with the flow, witness the source, your well spring of life, and feel the intensity of the waterfall as your spirit cascades magnificently forward, revealing every splendid droplet, withholding nothing.

Twenty-six rivers have melded with the ocean of life wherein lies humanity's collective dream insight. See not only your own reflection returned from this ocean's surface, but in reflection reach deeper, for it is beyond the surfaces and barriers which we believe exist that our wider reality is revealed.

This book has been a dip in that ocean. Still dripping with sea water, I see in my hand fast-fading memories, dream insights glimpsed throughout the creation of this manuscript, evaporating into the salty air as the sun hastens to dry my palm. The sun, symbolic of consciousness, absorbs and disperses droplets of the ocean, symbolic of the collective unconscious, for you to ponder as you continue your own journey:

*I don't believe we have to go through all this struggle and karma any more. I think things have changed to the point where we can live and come from a state of being in grace, and we can learn through joy and insight. If we can choose to learn through insight we don't need to go through struggle.*

ZOHARA

*… intellectually you understand something and say 'Yes, I know that', but it's not until you have that feeling that goes with it, or the actual understanding that you can do it. People can read it 'til they're blue in the face, but you need to feel it to know it. The difference is actually doing it in your life.*

SARRAS

*If I look at the painting now I can stand back and realise that life is a game, an illusion. The throw of the dice in any board game appear as the chance happenings in life which takes us up or down the snakes and ladders. Life is really a game, and if you can step back and see the whole board, you see life just takes us from the beginning to the end: and it's just a game.*

CALLI

*Now it doesn't matter what happens to me as I know it's only for my own growth and my own benefit so I go with it…I just see opportunities for growth. This attitude makes life a lot easier.*

ZOHARA

*In conclusion my life philosophy now is that it's actually not complicated at all! There is only really one thing: just be happy. The difference between being happy and unhappy is just basically deciding you're going to be happy. It's actually as simple as that. Simple, but not necessarily easy!*

VIOLET

*I realise now that it's all just a script you write yourself. We are just writing scripts until we finally learn, until we write (right) ourselves to the conclusion. It is all a dream and there is nothing but love.*

WRAITH

*My simple understanding is biblical: When God created the earth, so the Bible says, he spoke things into existence. We're supposed to be made in his image and I'm sure that if we can dream it, we can do it. If we can dream ourselves flying, then I'm sure we can achieve that.*

DANIEL

*We can say affirmations until we are blue in the face but we must simply be brainwashing the conscious mind. My dream had impact because my subconscious informed me of the emotional adjustment needed to achieve my conscious objective. All the conscious mind had to do was say 'Yes, I'll do it'.*

BETH

*People overlook the power of dreaming and take it for granted as something that we do. We're brought up thinking that we just have dreams and not to take it seriously, but, if you're really feeling in the dream, which a lot of people don't do, that's the key. Touch onto the feeling side of it.*

HARRY

*The general message for me has been to trust myself and go with what I want to do, to stop pushing aside my feelings and experiences... I have given up working in my old job, as it only served to stop me from being who I want to be...*

SUSANNAH

*I had to realise that I am the special person that I always wanted to be.*

WILLOW

*It was OK to be me. It was OK to be a little weird. Who wasn't? Did I expect perfection from other people? No. So, why punish myself to the point of annihilation because I wasn't either?*

MELL

*It's all about loving yourself. I could never come to grips with that before. I thought I liked myself pretty well, but until you come to that within yourself, you're incapable really of helping anyone else.*

SARRAS

*Is this the secret to curing all addictions — drugs, alcohol and so on? Funny thing is, dreaming doesn't cost a cent.*

BETH

*And even though we're not at the end of the tunnel yet, the fact is, we wouldn't be the same people we are now if we hadn't gone through this period of our lives. Neither would I be living my life with such an open mind or strong sense of wonderment.*

SUSANNAH

*I realise now, looking back at my journey, that no-one could do it for me. I had to do it for myself.*

SARRAS

*He reaches out towards the wall and shows me a miracle.*
*'See?', he says. 'It's all in your mind. If you don't like it this way,*
*you can make it better any time you decide. It's up to you.'*
*Suddenly the wall is a yellow and orange curtain, sliding sideways,*
*and all at once the whole room is flooded with sunlight. Finally*
*I understand with blinding clarity that it is all up to me. As soon*
*as I make up my mind to do it, I can free myself — pull open the*
*curtain, see outside, go out into freedom if I want. I'm the creator of*
*my own prison. It's only real because I've chosen to believe that it is.*
*The miracle is — it doesn't have to be that way at all!*

MELL

# Keeping a Dream Journal

## Instructions

1. Take a double-page spread for each day.
2. Record your dreams on the right-hand page.
3. Record the date (the date being the evening you went to bed).
4. Give every dream a title.
5. Don't worry if you can't recall the order of your dreams.
6. Write as much descriptive detail as you can remember, including your feelings and the emotional impact of the dreams.
7. Divide the left-hand page into two columns.
8. In one column, briefly record events, thoughts, conflicts, feelings, or questions of the day prior to sleep. (These may come into your dreams.)
9. In the other column, make notes on your associations to the dream, or any possible interpretations.
10. Use the last pages of your Dream Journal as an index so you can find the dreams easily.

## Left-hand page

| INTERPRETATIONS/ASSOCIATIONS | DAILY NOTES |
|---|---|
| 1. I had a pair of red shoes when I was ten.<br>I had my sights set high then.<br>2. The solid oak is not as it seems.<br><br>Perhaps I need to look towards the horizon, set a longer term goal. Things change. I should look beyond what appears to be secure, to what I really want to do. | *Monday 19 June 1995*<br>• A few knockbacks today.<br>• Losing sense of purpose.<br>• Am I on the right track? |

## Right-hand page

*Monday 19 June 1995*

1. Red Shoes on the Horizon

I looked through a telescope at a red dot on the horizon. It was a pair of red shoes; the most beautiful I have ever seen…

2. Oak Tree Disappears

A huge oak tree shimmered before me, like a mirage. A second later, it had vanished. I felt stunned, yet awed by such magic…

## Back pages

DREAM INDEX

*19 June 1995*
1. Red Shoes on the Horizon
2. Oak Tree Disappears

*20 June 1995*
1. Sliced Bread

*21 June 1995*
1. Ant wore Glasses
2. Visiting Aunt Em

# The Dream Research Bank

For information on:

* How to become involved in future research into dreams

* Receiving the Dream Research Bank's quarterly publication 'DreamNet'

* Staying informed

Write to:

The Dream Research Bank
PO Box 1735
Milton Business Centre
QLD 4064 Australia